FOR HIS OWN GOOD WILL AND PLEASURE

by Michael Forrest

ISBN 0 9546273 0 X

This edition published in Great Britain by
Michael Forrest

Printed in Great Britain by
Design Print Imagination Ltd – Tel: 01594 860504

To:

AMDG

CONTENTS

4

INTRODUCTION

'Life's a tale told by an idiot,
Full of sound and fury,
Signifying nothing.'

Shakespeare

Is it? Is there any point to it? Is it all a chaotic jumble, Shakespeare typed by monkeys? If there is any point, what is it? How does it all hang together? The electron microscope can let us see the individual bits of a single cell in motion; scientific analysis has made gigantic leaps forward: but what about philosophical synthesis?

With the exception of one remarkable 20th century philosopher (of whom more later), philosophy seems to have lost confidence in its ability to explain the nature of things and got itself into a rut from which it seeks escape down a number of blind alleys like existentialism, pragmatism and language. Nor is it only main stream academic philosophy that seems to have largely thrown in the sponge. The Christian churches seem to have looked at their shrinking numbers of fully committed supporters and also lost their self-confidence. When the doctrines that they preached in the way that they preached them seemed to carry less and less conviction to the younger generation of an age where science was making one great discovery after another the churches largely abandoned the attempt to preach what might be called hard doctrine. The task of digesting the discoveries of science, such as DNA and the interchangeability of energy and matter, and restating concepts and doctrine in a way which incorporates and accommodates them seems so far to have been too Herculean an undertaking for either philosophers or theologians. The pace of discovery has accelerated throughout this century, is accelerating and will go accelerating. Some measure of the size of the task facing the churches may be judged from the fact that the Catholic church has only just formally rehabilitated Galileo and acknowledged that that

5

the earth goes round the sun. There has been an awful lot of scientific work since then! Preaching and church effort nowadays tends to concentrate on issues such as justice and peace. This is wholly laudable as far as it goes, but of itself it is hardly likely to draw the missing millions back to the pews. After all, anybody with a strong conscience about social issues may well feel more drawn towards something like OXFAM or Shelter, which have such issues as their primary role. Social awareness is not enough on its own. To carry conviction to the scientifically aware younger generations the churches will have to carry intellectual conviction with their message in this modern age. I cannot – and certainly do not – claim to have all the answers – or even most of them. My hope is that by floating some hypotheses and posing some questions I can help to stimulate discussion and channel it in directions where others will continue it. Karl Marx has caused enormous suffering in the world through his wildly wrong ideas, but it seems to me that he was right in at least one of his ideas, that of the dialectic, where thesis generates antithesis and this results in a synthesis which becomes in its turn the next thesis. My aim is to start a new line of dialectic with a new thesis. If my tongue is occasionally in my cheek, as it sometimes will be, I hope it will not be too obvious because I want to stimulate and even annoy in the hope of provoking discussion and moving ideas along.

Philosophers have had a problem with tables for thousands of years. I do not mean astronomical tables or tide tables but pieces of furniture like the kitchen table and the dining table. Bertrand Russell spends the first chapter of his book on the problems of philosophy worrying about a table. Is it really there at all? Is what is there what our senses tell us is there? Do other people think that they see or feel the same thing that we think we see or feel? It looks different in different lights. It looks different from different directions. Is it really all in the mind? And so on. The object of all this is to show how difficult it is to be absolutely certain about anything at all. When Descartes tried this exercise his certainty was whittled down to one famous statement, "Cogito, ergo sum", "I am thinking, therefore I exist". It took Descartes an awfully long time sitting ruminating in his dressing gown to get even as far as this. I would like to look at some very extensive topics and life simply is not long enough to tackle them all to such philosophical depths. In any case my aim is not to make statements and prove them but to follow ideas and see where they lead. When faced with a choice I shall be unashamedly subjective and choose the alternative which appears to me to be the more reasonable.

Before trampling the grass of pastures new I need to describe the existing basis on which I intend to build. It is almost impossible to string two sentences together about even a straightforward subject without being misunderstood somewhere by somebody. So to have any chance at all of avoiding misunderstandings later on in the book it is absolutely vital that we should be 'on all fours', as the diplomats say, with regard to the building blocks. If we do not start from the same place there is no point in starting at all. There is a body of ideas thought out by other people which I have already accepted and I will begin by setting these out and describing briefly why I have accepted them. I shall not attempt to prove them. To the best of my knowledge nobody has ever managed to prove that my kitchen table is really there, or, if it is there, what it is. I shall simply describe these basic concepts and perhaps give some idea of why they seem reasonable to me. Some of them may seem to be BGOs (blinding glimpses of the obvious), but it is sometimes quite amazing what use can be made of them as building blocks. They also tend at times to be rather stodgy reading. However it is essential that they should be read or the danger of misunderstanding will become a certainty. Therefore I shall make an effort to adopt a conversational style. Indeed it is my intention throughout to avoid an academic style like the plague. Some of the material is difficult enough in itself without making it more difficult by the language used. I could take the cowards way out and wrap it all up in a package such that it would be impossible to be sure what I really meant, but that is not the object of the exercise. I want to reach an overall view that can be clearly understood in a way that can be clearly understood.

Pace Kant, I think that the reason why discussion has stalled is because everybody starts from inside space-time. The view from there has proved to be too restricted and the ground too shifting for it to be used as a suitable starting point. I shall therefore seek firmer ground on which to build by starting with absolutes outside space-time. This focusses and gives bounds to the discussion remarkably quickly. Let us therefore make a start on describing the basis on which I hope to make an essay at coherence.

THE BOTTOM LINE

A. THE EXISTENCE OF GOD

Setting out reasons for believing in the existence of God not only fulfils the obvious purpose but also paints in the first outlines of what it is that we believe in. If you asked a hundred people to describe their idea of God you would probably get a hundred and one different answers. It is therefore essential for this business of 'getting on all fours' to make it crystal clear just what sort of a God we are going to believe in. So as we set out reasons for why we should believe in anything at all we also start to lay foundations on which we can build and develop. I may say here and now that this chapter contains no original thinking of mine. The arguments in it are essentially unchanged since they were set out in detail by Thomas Aquinas some 700 years ago. All I shall try to do is give an outline of them, including in it what I need to draw on later on.

There is the rather tricky ontological argument for the existence of God as being the thing which you cannot conceive of anything greater than. But, however valid it might be, it does always seem to smack of philosophical sleight of hand and, what is more, it is not a very good building block. So I shall just outline some of what are called the cosmological arguments. They have this name because they look to the cosmos round about us for their starting point.

Let us begin with motion. All around us we see things moving, and what is moved is moved by another. Newton said words to the effect that a body at rest or in uniform motion in a straight line will continue in that state unless it is acted upon by an external force. This is obvious with an inanimate object like a football which cannot move at all unless somebody gives it a kick; but even living bodies, although they have some powers of self-motion, rely on other things for motion and change. For example, they must have food. Nothing has in itself the complete and sufficient reason for its motion. This follows from the nature of motion or change. What a thing has not got it cannot give to itself (BGO number one!) and so nothing that moves or changes can be the adequate cause of this. Everything that moves is moved by another and that other is in turn moved by another and so on and so on and so on. In the end there must be some being that produces the changes in the things that are moved but is itself unmoved and immovable, the First Immovable Mover. This is rather inescapable, because if the First Immovable Mover were moved he would have been moved by another and so would not be the full and sufficient reason for the changes in himself or in anything he moved. No matter how far back you take the series of movers, in the end there has to be a First Immovable Mover; and this being we call God.

Next let us look at efficient causality. In the world about us we can see effects which are caused. We can see creatures coming into being through the action of their parents. They then need other things to act on them to make them continue in existence, things like air and food and heat. If I am playing tennis the ball moves because I hit it with the racquet and the racquet moves because I swing it and I can swing it because I have eaten my weeties and so on and so on. The thing is that all the causes acting in our experience are secondary, dependent ones, that is, they only cause in so far as they have been caused by something else. Just as in the case of motion, if we follow the causes back we must come in the end to a First Uncaused Cause, a being who causes all the secondary causes but is himself uncaused. We have to come back to a being who is not dependent either for his existence or his causality upon any other cause whatsoever and who is the source of the existence of the causality of all the secondary, dependent causes. This First Uncaused Cause we call God.

Thirdly, let us look at contingency. All around us we see contingent beings. By a contingent being I mean something that does not exist necessarily. It exists but it can not-exist. It comes into being and it can cease to be what it is. It does not exist of necessity. Existence is not of its essence. Living things are born and die. All life on earth had a beginning at some point in history. Inanimate bodies also change; they are broken up and recombine; they do not exist neces-

10

sarily. Contingent beings can be or not be. They cannot account for their own existence. And if each individual one cannot account for its own existence then neither can the some total of them all. An analogous example is that a room full of blind people does not add up to one person with sight. So where did the contingent beings get their existence from? As they do not exist of themselves they must have been given existence by another; and ultimately, in a similar way to the cases of motion and cause, we must come to a being who gives life but does not receive it, who exists of himself necessarily and as part of his essence and is the source of existence for all contingent beings. This self-existent, non-contingent, necessary being we call God.

Finally, let us look at design or order. Let us ignore for now that for the world to get here at all there has to be an Immovable Mover, an Uncaused Cause. Let us look at the world around us as it is. We see an amazing design or order, both in individual things and in the relations between things. Without labouring the point, let us look for a start at something very small, the atom. I shall look at it according to Bohr theory, as I am not very well up in Laplacians. But in any case the end result seems to be much the same. I remember my science master saying that when he was at university electrons had mass on Mondays and Wednesdays and were solely energy on Tuesdays and Thursdays. Anyway, whether it is a precise orbit or an area of wave motion the fact remains that in the one nearest to the nucleus there can be 2 electrons, in the next one out there can be 8, in the next one out there can be 18, then 32, then 50. The maximum number of electrons in each orbit is $2n^2$, where n is the principal quantum number, the number of the ring out from the nucleus. This applies to every single atom. What is more, each atom of a given element is precisely the same as all the myriad of other atoms of the same element. That is just one simple example and there are plenty more to be seen if we look at the world round about us. They do say that, given a typewriter and sufficient time and paper, a monkey would eventually type out the whole of Shakespeare; but no way would he type it out with precise accuracy again and again and again and again. That is the difference.But order requires an intelligent orderer. To produce order requires intelligence. Unintelligent beings cannot produce order of themselves because they are indifferent to either acting or not acting or to acting in one way rather than another; and so their actions have to be directed by someone else. That someone else knows the end to be attained and orders and directs the movements and actions of the unintelligent agents as means to that end. A packet of wheels and springs and screws can only become a watch by the direction of an intelligent man. In the same way, any order, any movement to an end requires an intelligent mover; all order requires an orderer. So the order in the world, in things themselves and between things, requires a supreme, intelligent orderer and this orderer we call God.

Let me give the final word on this subject to Abbe Verhelst. "The one who puts order into things is perforce also the orderer of their being. For if all nature is ordered towards its end by the play of native tendencies, then it ought to have received those native tendencies at the same time as its limited kind of being. The orderer of the world is identified therefore with the supreme cause of all that exists."

As I said at the beginning of this chapter, there is no original thought from me here. I have drawn heavily on my school notes from many moons ago. I have not set out to prove the existence of God beyond any possible dispute but simply to outline some of the arguments which make it seem more reasonable to me to accept such existence than not to do so, and in setting out these arguments to begin to give some sort of form, dimension or quality – call it what you will – to this being commonly known as God. At this fork in the road towards progress in knowledge I turn away from the branch marked 'No God' and set off down the one marked 'God'. The next step is to see where we are lead by the acknowledgement of an Immovable Mover, an Uncaused Cause, a self-existent necessary being and a supreme intelligent orderer.

12

B. THE ATTRIBUTES OF GOD

We cannot know God directly, but this does not mean that we cannot know anything at all about him. Some of the things that God must be were set out when going through the reasons for believing in his existence. We can go on from there to say something of what God is not. We find that the things of the world are in many ways imperfect and it is because of their imperfections that they cannot account for themselves. So we know that God does not have these imperfections. We can think of the perfections of God in a negative way, excluding from him the imperfections of creatures. They are finite, changeable, compound; God is infinite, immutable, simple.

There are two main tools I would like to use for listing, once again with a brief statement of reasons, some of the more important attributes of God. The first tool is analysis of what is implied in the Necessary Being that was mentioned in the contingency argument. The second is consideration of God as the sole primary cause, the First Uncaused Cause.

The First Uncaused Cause cannot have been produced by another and so it must exist of itself. In the same way, the First Immovable Mover cannot have received any perfection from another and so has not received existence; it exists of itself. Again, the absolutely necessary being must exist necessarily and so it is independent of any other in existence, existing of itself – *ens a se*, as scholars would put it. God then exists of himself. In his essence he has the sufficient reason for his existence. His very nature is to be in complete and infinite fulness of being. As the Necessary Being, the First Uncaused Cause has none of the imperfections of contingent, caused things; it has the complete fulness of being and is the sole *raison d'etre* of all things real or possible. The Necessary Being contains virtually all that is.

Here I must add a word of explanation about what I mean by 'virtually'. When I say that the Necessary Being contains virtually all that is I do not mean that it contains 'nearly' all that is. I am using 'virtually' in the sense derived from its root word *virtus* in the sense

13

of force or power. The Necessary Being contains the power within itself to produce all that is; it is the cause of all things.

We normally divide things up into essence and attributes. The essence of a thing is what it primarily and fundamentally is; while the attributes are the other qualities which it has in addition to or resulting from its essence. For example, the essence of man is that he is a rational animal and his attributes are such things as size, colour, co-ordination, patience and so on. In a creature there are thus many attributes which are not identical with the essence. God, however, is simple, by which I mean that God cannot be made up of parts and is incapable of division. If God were to be made up of parts, then these parts are either finite or infinite. If they are finite, then a number of finites can never make an infinite. The parts cannot be infinite because it is impossible by definition to have more than one infinite. So if we take a purist line, there can be no distinction between the essence and attributes of God; but there is one aspect of the perfection of God which perhaps strikes us as the most fundamental and from which we can most easily go on to consider other aspects, so it is convenient to speak of it as the divine essence. This essence is the fulness of being with no limitation. It is Subsistent Being.

If we look at the existence of creatures we see that it is not perfect. The qualities of creatures, technically known as accidents (e.g. height), are more easily changeable than the substance of a creature; but contingent beings in all their aspects receive a measure of existence and when that measure is used up they cease to exist. We have to remove these imperfections of existence from our idea of God's existence. He must exist in himself and of himself. As he is not contingent but necessary, he must exist necesarily. His essence is identical with his existence; he exists essentially; his existence is unlimited; he is existence. As the scholars would put it, he is *ipsum esse per se subsistens*. This is recorded with remarkable force and clarity in Exodus, where God's description of himself is given as "I am who am" – I am Being, my essence is to be. This is what I mean by subsistent being. Please note that I do not say that God is *the* Subsistent Being, but that God is Subsistent Being.

Now let us move on to some attributes of God which may come in useful during thinking further on down the line. This part may be full of apparent BGOs because the same or similar reasons crop up again and again, but please bear with me because some of it at least will be useful for future reference.

We have already noted that God is Simple and Infinite. God is also One because we cannot have two infinites. One infinite could only be distinguishable from the other by the presence of a perfection in one which was lacking in the other; but by definition an infinite has the fulness of being or perfection and cannot lack a perfection. There is only room for one infinite and so God is One. Similarly he is Perfect, i.e. complete and lacking in nothing. If we go back for a moment to the idea of the First Immovable Mover, we were talking of a being which brings about all change and yet is not changed or moved by another, which is the source of all activity and is always in action. Its activity is identical with itself, pure act. There is no passing from not acting to acting as there is in secondary movers. It does not become something it was not; it is its acts. It is pure act.

Next, as the Necessary Being God is without beginning and without end. Furthermore his existence must be without succession because this involves change and is applicable only to a changeable subject, not to one already perfect. A thing which exists in time has lost the existence of the past and has not yet had the existence of the future. Being perfect, God's existence has to be without the succession of parts, without division into past, present and future, a full unchanging measureless existence, one unchanging NOW. The quality of Eternity was defined by Boethius as *interminabilis vitae tota simul et perfecta possessio* – possession of life without beginning or end, pefectly and as a simultaneous whole.

Without labouring things I think that at this stage I can simply state that as the source of everything God has infinite knowledge or omniscience and has absolute power or omnipotence. Finally. as a

15

source of the limited personality in man, God possesses personality freed from all limitations or defects. His acts are those of his own will; anything else would be incompatible with infinite perfection.

One could go on defining more attributes but the ones mentioned so far will probably suffice. It has been rather a stodgy chapter, even though I have skated over things in a way which can only be described as sketchy. The whole concept of God is so awe-inspiring that we tend to take refuge in a cosy mental picture of a dear old gentleman with a long beard wearing a long white robe and sitting on a cloud. I am afraid that just will not do. To approach space-time from the outside we must recognise the enormity of God and keep this idea in mind if our perspective is to be meaningful.

THE BIBLE STORY

What interests me primarily in the Bible, both Old and New Testaments, as the final plank in the foundation platform on which to build my mental house of cards is the Bible as a historical document. Sizeable chunks of the Old Testament are made up of things like psalms and proverbs, but my prime interest in it is as a historical account of the progress of the Jewish people. Similarly, the Gospels are an account of the life of Christ, while the Acts of the Apostles and Epistles give some narrative of the early Christian church.

I take the Old Testament from the point where Abraham takes centre stage as a historical narrative in the same spirit in which I accept Xenophon's account of the march of the 10,000 or Caesar's account of his campaigns in Gaul. The Israelites were evidently a people who took the compilation of social records seriously and it seems reasonable to accept their historical narrative as being reasonably accurate. Because of the time covered, the source narrative must have been the work of many authors initially, even if all the books were later collated and edited by individual authors or groups of authors. Through much of this work there is a continual interplay with God, who revealed himself to Abraham as "I am who am", and who is usually referred to as Yahweh. I shall follow this convention and refer to God in the context of the Old Testament as Yahweh. It never ceases to amaze me that so many thousand years ago, long before anybody had ever put forward the Big Bang theory, the origin of the cosmos and the evolution of earth and life on earth are set out just as modern science has reconstructed it: the Big Bang, the formation of planet earth, the settling down to land and sea, the evolution of plants then fish then birds then animals then man. The whole story is there in a few short sentences and in the right order, as we now know. No creation story of any other region or religion that I know of holds a candle to it as a scientific and factual description of what happened. The Greeks had Time marrying Earth and producing various children, all of them gods. The Japanese had Izanagi dipping his lance into the sea and the drops that fell off became the islands of Japan. Yet Genesis, thousands of years ago, starts right at the beginning by saying that all was void and then God said, "Let there be light" – let there be the Big Bang. The thought of it is enough to give one a *frisson*. I find myself unable to believe that the authors of the creation legends of the Fertile Crescent, which are the source for the first chapters of Genesis, could have thought out for themselves and set down in a few short sentences what it has taken countless eminent philosophers and scientists thousands of years to re-establish. The only conclusion I can draw for myself is that the authors had help, though in what form I would not like to hazard a guess. The Old Testament is a very special book. It is full of Yahweh and the Israelites were aware of themselves as a special people, the chosen race. This was an additional incentive to keep a good record of their history, in addition to all the requirements of tribal custom and of the establishment of kinship and ownership.

The New Testament is of modern origin compared with something like Genesis. It is about times nearer to ours than those of Julius Caesar. I have no problem in accepting the fact that there was a man called Julius Caesar; that he invaded Gaul; and that that country was then divided into three parts. In a similar way I have no inherent problem in accepting that there was a person called Christ; that the Gospels give an account of his life; and that the Epistles and Acts of the Apostles are about the early Christian church.

There are in fact certain criteria which we apply consciously or unconsciously to a greater or lesser extent before we accept the facts narrated in any historical document. We have to be satisfied about three things, namely, the *authenticity* or genuineness of the document i.e. that it is written by the author to whom it is ascribed, the *veracity* of the author i.e. that he or those to whom he spoke witnessed the events and that he narrated them faithfully and the *integrity* of the document i.e. that the original text has remained substantially unchanged. If we are satisfied on all these points we can accept the facts narrated. Almost invariably we accept the word of somebody else. I accept that Julius Caesar was murdered on the Ides of March even though I have done no research into that sad event myself. My teacher told me – and even he was simply passing on knowledge which had been researched by earlier scholars. It would not really be any more unreasonable to accept the New Testament as a historical document than it would be to accept Caesar's Gallic Wars. They have both been accepted as such by countless generations. However, as the Gospels impinge much more on modern daily life and thought than Caesar's Gallic Wars, it may be of interest to give a brief outline of more specific reasons for acceptance as historical documents, at least for the case of the Gospels – the reasons why they have been so accepted by the research scholars on whose authority the rest of us rely.

The most important early researcher, who set his findings down in writing, is St.Irenaeus. He was born in the East, spent two periods in Rome and in AD 180 was Bishop of Lyons in Gaul. Tertullian said that Irenaeus was athirst for knowledge of all kinds. He collected reports of the early ecclesiastical authorities almost back to the very beginning so that he would be able to quote the oldest traditions against the Gnostics. He was himself a disciple of St.Polycarp, the Bishop of Smyrna, who had known St.John and other disciples personally. In his work *Adversus Haereses* he writes, 'Matthew published his Gospel among the Hebrews and in their language at the time when Peter and Paul were preaching the glad tidings in Rome and founding the church there. After their decease, Mark also, the pupil and interpreter of Peter, has given us what had been preached by Peter. Luke, however, a companion of Paul, has chronicled in his work the Gospel as it was preached by that Apostle. After that, John, the Disciple of the Lord who reclined upon His breast, published his Gospel also while he was residing at Ephesus in Asia.' Other celebrated scholars of the same period include Clement of Alexandria, Origen and Eusebius. Origen was a famous biblical scholar and the author of 2,000 books. He wrote, 'I have learned from tradition that the four Gospels recognised without contradiction throughout the whole

19

church, throughout the whole world, were written by Matthew, Mark, Luke and John.' These men and the other scholars of the time could trace their line of teachers back to the Apostles and earliest disciples. Other spurious Gospels, such as the so-called Gospel to the Hebrews and Gospel of St.Mathias, were not accepted. Also, evidence in a negative sort of way is provided by the Jews, who would have denied the authenticity if they could, but they did not. Nor did the pagans deny the Apostolic origin. Celsus in AD 178 attacked Christianity but referred to the Gospels as 'the written stories of the Disciples'.

The text of the Gospels shows that the authors were Jews and contemporaries or disciples of contemporaries of the events. They used a sort of Greek based on Aramaic which was used by Jewish writers of the 1st century and not later. They incorporated Hebrew terms and idioms. They showed no acquaintance with Greek philosophy or literature but they had an intimate knowledge of Jewish customs and religion and the Old Testament writings. The Jewish world changed in both its religious and political aspects after the destruction of Jerusalem by the Romans in AD 70. We find the life of pre-AD 70 in the Gospels. The destruction of Jerusalem is still a prophecy. The narrative has a vividness and detail which indicates personal experience of the events; and the general historical accuracy is confirmed by non-Christian writers of the period such as Josephus.

Let us turn now to the veracity of the Evangelists – whether they knew the facts and reported them faithfully. As we have seen in the earlier quotation from Irenaeus, Matthew and John were Apostles; Mark was the pupil and interpreter of Peter; and Luke was the companion of Paul. As to whether or not they gave a true account, the obvious thing is that it would have been pointless for them to give an untrue account. From different motives, both the disciples of Christ and the enemies of Christ would have exposed any attempt to give an untruthful account.

Finally, let us look very briefly at the integrity of the Gospels. The originals would have been written on papyrus, a perishable material. We know from Pope Clement (AD 95–98) that they were written down and that they were in constant use, being read in all the churches. There must have been a large number of manuscript copies. Indeed, it is reckoned that at the end of the 2nd century, the time of the most ancient surviving text, there were more than 60,000 copies. We must also remember that variation between copies would have been made more difficult in those days by the strong tradition of learning important books by heart because many people either could not read or did not have enough money to commission their own copy. The scriptures were cared for by a special body of men called Lectors and preserved in the house of the Bishop. It therefore seems reasonable to accept that the integrity of the Gospels is established at least as well as that of other historical books.

I have given above a thumbnail sketch of why I find it reasonable to accept the Gospels as historical documents – and for similar sorts of reasons the Epistles and Acts of the Apostles as well. Some idea of the reasons may have proved to be of interest; but it would not be too unreasonable simply to accept such very widely accepted works in the same way as we do those of Caesar or Livy or Herodotus or Xenophon.

THOUGHT AND ACTION

An elderly relative of mine was wont to say, "I wish I could be in bed without the bother of having to get there." Unfortunately, thinking about being about being in bed is not enough. I have to rouse myself from a comfortable chair by the warm fireside, walk upstairs, get undressed and hang my clothes up, put on my pyjamas and pull back the bedclothes before finally climbing into bed. As a friendly gesture to somebody we may sometimes say that we will take the will for the deed; but in that case the deed itself remains undone. If I want to do something as simple as kicking a football I still have to run up to it, balance on one leg with the knee slightly bent, swing the other leg down so that the boot kicks the ball, at the same time straightening up the first leg to give added impetus.

Thought has to be translated into action by the physical part of us. At least, that is so in most cases. It does not seem necessarily to be always so. There seem to be some non-material things where the thought and the action are not separated. For example, I do not have to make any physical action to be angry or to hate somebody. If I think, "I hate you", I am doing the act. I am hating you.

From such an example it may be possible for us to frame some analogous idea of what happens in the case of Subsistent Being. Perhaps it would be a good idea if I made clear just what I mean by analogical knowledge. We use three kinds of names for things, univocal, equivocal and analogous. A univocal name is one which is always used in the same sense (e.g. man, animal). An equivocal name is used in senses which are entirely different (e.g. sleeper, vice). An analogous name is used in senses which are partly the same and partly different (e.g. healthy as used of man, clothing, complexion; cause as used of man and pen in writing). If what is expressed by the name is something which is to be found in each of the things of which it is used but in different ways or degrees (e.g. cause in the above example) then the name is analogous with an analogy of proportionality. If what is expressed by the name is only in one of the things of which it is used and is only atttributed to the others because of their relationship to that one, then the name is analogous with an analogy of attribution (e.g. healthy in the above example). So we may be able to form some impression analogically from our own experience. We have a material side and a non-material side to us, but, even in our own case, thought and action are not separated for non-material things such as emotions. We have seen that Subsistent Being is pure act and possesses virtually (as ever, this word is used in the sense of having the power to cause) anything that there could possibly be. If Subsistent Being thinks something then, by virtue of the very fact that he thinks it, it is. Thought and action are inseparable. It is a THINK-ACT. Every thought of Subsistent Being is a think-act.

As Subsistent Being is pure action and as he is also infinite, he will be carrying out an infinite number of think-acts. Infinity is not something of which we can easily have even an analogous knowledge. It might be of help towards obtaining some fleeting impression of what is meant by infinity if I quote a well used illustration couched in terms within our experience which relates in fact to infinite time, eternity. Imagine a steel ball so big that it reaches out to the furthest star you can see. Imagine that once in every million years a bird flies by and brushes this steel ball with its wingtip. When that enormous steel ball has been completely worn away, all the aeons that have passed by make no impression at all on eternity. It is not a very satisfactory illustration at all, but if we take the idea across to acts, to the think-acts of Subsistent Being, then we may have the first glimmerings of an inkling of the enormity of their numbers.

Could I now suggest that a think-act of Subsistent Being is brought about by the application of an infinitesimal part of his infinite power. In our experience, power is related to energy in some form or other, but we really have no idea of the nature of divine power. We only know by its effect that it has the ability to cause.

So we have this myriad of applications of infinitesimal amounts of divine power, of think-acts of Subsistent Being, and one of them was, "Let there be light". There is an awful lot contained in that simple-looking idea. Light is in the form of a regular wave motion and so it has velocity; it moves through a certain distance in a set interval. Light is thus the governing parameter of space-time. But we can also think of light as a result of the power of the divine think-act, the emanation from the explosion of divine power. We even have that sort of idea ourselves in the common saying, "It came to me in a flash". Light is an expression of the power of the think-act in terms of energy. Philosophers sought for a long time to discover the stuff of the universe. Their ideas progressed with science, but when Leibnitz was ready to arrive at the truth he was too far ahead of the science of his day. There was no way of expressing scientifically what he was trying to say. Leibnitz argued that complex things are made up of simpler things and that ultimately one comes down to the simplest possible components from which everything else is aggregated. Without an electron microscope and modern technology Leibnitz was only able to argue in the direction of atoms and the particles that make them up. Yet he went even further. He devised a thing called a monad. He argued that anything that occupies space is extended and is therefore divisible. The ultimate stuff of the world had to be non-extended and thus non-material. The world had to be made up of a huge number of non-material, metaphysical points. Living in the late 1600s, Leibnitz had enormous problems taking his line of thought further. He really needed to talk about energy, but he was too far ahead of his time. When Schopenhauer came along nearly two hundred years later he argued that matter is fixed energy, that in principle all matter must be able to be converted into energy and that a material object is a space filled with force. About a hundred years later physics provided the scientific details to bear out this notion; and Einstein linked the totality together in his famous equation $\Sigma = MC^2$.

Somehow or other some of the expanding surge of energy came to be fixed as matter. I have seen a theory that eddies developed in the light waves and the concentration of photons deepened until the quantum of energy was enough to produce the first and simplest at-

24

oms, the hydrogen and helium of the stars. I remember seeing a New Scientist article which said that new stars were apparently still appearing, as if dripping from the framework of space-time. The evolution of all that is material went on from there. What we must not lose sight of is that this was not just an act that created energy and matter: it was a think-act. The energy and matter are just manifestations of the power of the idea encapsulated and evolving in the think-act. That is perhaps the tricky bit for us. We are used to separating energy, matter and consciousness, but that it because of our limitations. Subsistent Being has no such limitations. Everything here is the result of the encapsulation of one idea, albeit encapsulating a format permitting change and evolution, because God also established the laws that govern its development. It is all one think-act, one application in an innumerable myriad of applications of divine power.

Perhaps I ought to make it clear here that I am not postulating an enormous number of parallel worlds. We are limited in our imagination; Subsistent Being is not. There is no reason at all why any other think-act should bear any resemblance at all to the one that has produced our cosmos. It may be, of course, that Subsistent Being has executed other think-acts similar to ours but with a range of variations in the parameters. However, there is no need to repeat yourself if you have infinite power and infinite imagination. Every other think-act may be so different that we cannot even begin to imagine it. All we can have experience of is the think-act in which we find ourselves,

And what a think-act it is! Snowflakes and the United Nations and wool. Stained glass windows and the song of the thrush and oak trees. Birds feathers and silk worms and newspapers. Glue and the howl of a storm and flames. Computers and milk and Disneyland. Mozart's music and Shakespeare's plays. Mud and the smell of curry and rugby. One could go on and on. What an astonishing variety! What a think-act! This, I would suggest, is what is really contained in that deceptively simple little sentence of four words, "Let there be light".

Now that we have put ourselves in perspective let us go on to think about things from inside our think-act. But we must never lose the sense of perspective while we do so. I recently read of a theory that God was a projection of our imagination. What a preposterous, unbalanced idea! However could contingent beings, no matter how many in number, create the one essential necessary being. A quick reference back to contingency as a reason for accepting the existence of God very quickly shows such an idea to be rubbish. That sort of thing shows the danger of starting to look at things from where we are, from inside space-time. That is why I have stayed outside space-time so far in order to set out the fundamentals and establish the perspectives. We have them ready to refer back to as a yardstick. Now let us go on into space-time.

EVOLUTION FROM LIGHT TO THOUGHT

We have then a stupendous think-act which burst into existence with the Big Bang. The power of the idea showed itself as light, a form of electromagnetic radiation. We think of light as energy, but even light has a certain granularity. Einstein introduced the concept of the photon in 1905 so as to make it possible to give a satisfactory quantitative explanation of some of the properties of electromagnetic radiation which could not be dealt with adequately in terms of wave theory. This photon is an elementary constituent of electromagnetic radiation moving with the speed of light and having particle properties. Photons are believed to have zero mass when at rest. The energy E of a photon of frequency v is given by $E = hv$ (where h is Planck's constant). So a photon is an electromagnetic quantum and electromagnetic radiation is discontinuous, existing as a set of photons. This certainly helped Einstein in quantitative studies of photoelectric effect, but it is singularly difficult to comprehend a particle which has zero mass. Be that as it may, it is a first step in a granularity which has observably developed. By whatever means it happened, energy was fixed in the transient reservoirs of material particles, nuclei and electrons, the first atoms. These became further aggregated into clouds of atoms and into the stars of the galaxies. Some of the matter from our own sun was sucked off by the gravitational pull of another large object passing by and so the planets were formed. The small size of the planets has lead to relatively rapid cooling, so that we now have the earth as it is today with a solid, cool crust and a hot fluid core.

As the earth cooled down, basic particles combined in ever more complex and intricate forms. We can observe the action of an in-built law in the Think-act for the progressive occurrence of complexification.The whole range of the atomic table was formed and not only atoms but molecules like the water of the sea and the ores in which the metals are lodged. Yet when we look even at this it is not straightforward at all. It seemed that the coming of appliances like the electron microscope would allow us to see things in such detail that all the secrets of science and philosophy might be revealed. However, the capability for ever more detailed analysis turns out to be sterile in that respect. It leads downwards to molecules, atoms, sub-atomic particles and eventually to electrons and photons. Once we get down to a certain level everything loses its individuality and turns into a mass of particles. Yet the things in the world around us are clearly more than heaps of identical bits and pieces. Each identifiable non-simple thing has a collective unity. The range of matter as we know it is not simply an aggregation and juxtaposition of atoms. An identity absorbs and cements them together. And, just as each particle fits into its own small system, each system fits into a larger system and all systems have their place in the total system of the universe.

What I must do without further delay is to make a necessary digression and acknowledge the debt which I owe for some of the fundamental and essential ideas expressed in this essay to the man whom I mentioned at the beginning of the book, the man who in my estimation is by far the greatest philosopher of the 20th century and one of the great philosophers of all time, Pierre Teilhard de Chardin. He was born in 1881 near Clermont in the mountainous region of the Massif Central in France. At the age of 18 he entered the Jesuit noviciate and when he had completed his studies, including philosophy and theology, some six years later he was sent to Cairo to teach physics. He himself was at this time primarily a geologist. Perhaps it was the antiquities of Egypt that stimulated his interest in paleontology. From Cairo he came to Hastings in Sussex for his final theology studies between 1909 and 1912, when he was ordained priest. During the First World War he served as a stretcher bearer with such calm gallantry under the heaviest fire the he was awarded the Military Medal and the Legion of Honour. After the war he became Professor of Geology at the Catholic Institute in Paris and took his Doctorate at the Sorbonne in 1922. He went to China on his first paleontological mission in 1923 for a year but he found on his return to Paris that some of the ideas which he had expressed in his lectures on evolution worried his superiors. He was forbidden to continue teaching. He returned to China in 1926 and stayed there for almost the whole of the next 20 years. He worked as scientific adviser to the Geological Survey of China and took part in many expeditions, including the one which unearthed the skull of Peking man. His reputation as a paleontologist was such that in 1938 he was appointed Director of the Laboratory of Advanced Studies in Geology and Paleontology in Paris, but the outbreak of the Second World War prevented him from taking up this appointment. All this time he was not only writing scientific papers but also writing philosophically on evolution, but he was forbidden to publish this work. On his return to France he was forbidden to forward his candidature for a Professorship in the College de France, which would have been open to him, but he was made a Membre de L'Insitut, an Officer of the Legion d'Honneur and a Director of Research in the Centre Nationale de la Recherche Scientifique. His last years were spent in America and he died there in 1955. Always true to his vow of obedience, this remarkable polymath never published his philosophical works, but on his death they were quickly published by his friends and admirers. His most famous philosophical writings are tailored to different standpoints. In his most famous work, 'The Phenomenon of Man', he wrote as a scientist and natural philosopher. His correspondence from China adds in some measure a spiritual dimension which he excluded from his scientific work. 'Le Milieu Divin', on the other hand, expresses his views as a Catholic priest on the meaning and future of evolution. The scope of his vision is amazing, absolutely unprecedented. Unfortunately, the verbal means of communicating it barely existed. His position is somewhat analogous to that of Leibnitz's need of a way of describing energy before it had been discovered. The result is that his work makes difficult reading. One is reminded of Aristophanes's description of the works of Aeschylus as 'volleys of firmly bolted words'. The ideas were so grand and so complex and so innovative that expression of them was problematical. My only consolatory advice to anyone tackling 'The Phenomenon of Man' is to keep on to the end then start again at the beginning because by the third reading you should begin to have quite a good idea of what de Chardin is driving at. It was reading 'The Phenomenon of Man' that put into my mind the germ of the idea of writing this essay.

Taking up the narrative again from where I was before giving a brief introduction to Teilhard de Chardin, the whole system emanated from the Big Bang and is ongoing. What is evident as we look at it is a continuous and developing 'complexification'. Molecules become bigger until at last they reach the size at which we find viruses and bacteria and the building blocks for plant and animal life. What struck de Chardin while inspecting this progress was that as the units and arangement of units grew in complexity they eventually allowed the manifestation of an ever increasing consciousness. This is a line of thought that I would now like to develop.

Let us have a look first in this chapter at the easy part of evolution. By this I mean the part that can be observed scientifically, albeit we have missed for ever the chance to observe the earlier part at first hand. Nevertheless we can form quite a good idea of what happened from what we can observe now and from what has been found from bygone ages.

The temperature in the stars is extremely high! It is too high to permit the occurrence of matter in anything but the most simple forms, like hydrogen and helium. The cooling of the earth, on the other hand, allowed the formation of more complex substances than are possible in the incandescent stars. And form they certainly did! As has been mentioned already it is as though there was a compulsion towards synthesis which was waiting for the opportunity to come to fruition. A most favourable region for this was near the earth's crust. The earth's core is the hot, fluid metal of the barysphere. Out in the rarefied cold of the stratosphere beyond the tropopause there is only a thin scattering of ions. It is in the ground, the water and the troposphere near the surface of the earth that the most favourable conditions for complexification occurred. As we come up to the earth's crust we find the silicates like granite and basalt. On the surface we have zones of water and air and carbonic acid enclosing the lithosphere within the hydrosphere and atmosphere. This area around the surface of the globe is the interesting one as it is the zone of progress. As the temperature decreased it allowed the formation of different elements and their combination in the earth's crust into a richly diversified mineral world. This is richly diversified, yet even so it is limited by the structure of its constituents. This applies even to the relatively numerous silicates. If we think of the minerals in terms of biological evolution we can say that they have come to the end of the road on which they set out. They cannot become bigger and more complex. They can indeed become just bigger by condensing down into crystals, but this is just a mosaic of small pieces without true union. This is what happened to most of the matter in the earth. It became more complex to the extent of forming into all the atoms and forming limited molecular structures. Had that been all that happened, we would not be here now. Fortunately for the progress of evolution, some elements took a different path. Instead of crystallisation they went on to polymerisation.

As most people are more than a little vague about organic chemistry, it may be helpful if I put in here a textbook explanation of what polymerisation is. It is a chemical union of two or more molecules of the same compound to form larger molecules, resulting in the formation of a new compound of the same empirical formula but of greater molecular weight. (The empirical formula is the simplest type of chemical formula, which only gives the proportion of each element present but does not give any indication of the molecular weight or molecular structure e.g. paraldehyde is $(CH_3CHO)_3$ and it is formed by the polymerisation of acetaldehyde, CH_3CHO, which is its empirical formula.) This is called 'addition polymerisation' and was the original meaning of the term. One now also refers to 'condensation polymerisation' in which the monomer (a compound of single molecules) molecules are joined by condensation into a polymer molecule, resulting in a different empirical formula, and

31

'copolymerisation' in which the polymer molecule is built up from two or more different kinds of monomer molecules. This is the world of organic chemistry. These are organic compounds. The three most important elements involved by far are carbon, hydrogen and oxygen, all of which abound in the regions of the hydrosphere and atmosphere. It is truly amazing what a range of substances and what a range of different properties can be obtained by various combinations of these three elements. Just two examples will illustrate this. C_2H_5OH is alcohol. $CH_2:C(CH_3)COOCH_3$ is methyl methacrylate and the polymerised form of this is perspex. Two very different substances, but both made up of the same three elements! Hardly surprisingly, another element which figures largely in organic compounds is nitrogen, another abundant element in the surface regions. Other elements, e.g. silicon, also find a place in some organic cmpounds. Organic chemistry was originally so named because it was the chemistry of substances produced by living organisms, as distinct from the inorganic chemistry of substances of mineral origin. It is essentially the chemistry of carbon compounds.

The scale and complexity of these polymerised organic compounds can be enormous. The atomic weight of hydrogen is 1, that of carbon is 12, that of nitrogen is 14 and that of oxygen is 16, but organic compounds can have molecular weights of over 1,000,000. This is the sort of scope for complexification which was not available to mineral development. And it is organic macromolecules that we find as the essential constituents of the next step up and on and outwards in evolution, living organisms.

It does not concern us in this straightforward narrative of evolution to consider how macromolecules 'came alive'. Macromolecules found in the living state in nature can be synthesised in the laboratory but they have defied attempts to give them life. Louis Pasteur, for one, tried hard but without success. Nevertheless the fact is that some of them did 'come alive' – or else we would not be here. It seems debatable whether or not a virus is animate or inanimate. They are so small you need an electron microscope to see them. The simplest ones are no more than a strand of ribonucleic acid coated with protein molecules. They can only increase and multiply by courtesy of a host cell - and they are not well behaved guests. When we go on to bacteria, however, we do seem to have crossed the borderline and come firmly into the realms of the animate world. Bacteria are usually single cells and reproduce by cell division or mitosis.

The best thing we can say about the start of life is that it begins with the cell. As the atom is the granule of matter, the cell is the natural granule of life. It is the natural building block for living things and indeed its behaviour as it becomes joined in ever larger structures with like cells and different cells makes one think of polymerisation and copolymerisation in the inanimate organic compounds.

So we find this film around the earth teeming with simple unicellular life; but, acting under a similar compulsion as did the atoms, the cells set off along the path of complexification. We can see the flowering of different levels of this complexification and they have by now been well mapped out. There is, however, an insurmountable problem in detecting the start of a new direction in the family tree of life. The first stages of a transformation would naturally have a minimum of differentiation and small numbers. By the time the new species or phylum has become established, the first fleeting stages of it have been obliterated by the passage of time. As de Chardin says, time, like a draughtsman with an eraser, rubs out every weak line in the drawing of life. He calls this the suppression of the peduncles. What this means, and it is more and more the case the further back in time we go, is that what we have knowledge of is the full flowering of a particular movement towards complexification. Indeed, if we use this metaphor in connection with the very earliest ages we might say that what we find is the overblown state. If we go back over 200 million years to the Permian era we are in the age of the primitive amphibians, the time when living things emerged from the waters which had up till then contained all living beings. The only traces are of already highly differentiated creatures, signifying that the development in this direction was coming to an end. Fortunately, from somewhere among the amphibians of the Permian times came a transformation that resulted in the theromorphs, the lords of the land in the Triassic times from 150 to 200 million years ago. Yet even by the end of the Triassic period there are thought to have been the first mammals, tiny rat-like animals. They were quite overshadowed during the following Jurassic period by the dinosaurs, the full bloom of reptiles, some of which went on eventually to produce the birds. The ramifications of a type in full bloom produce herbivores, insectivores, carnivores and omnivores to form a verticillate group with the same origins and which are mutually auxiliary and complementary. We have been left with good example of this in modern times in the marsupials of Australia. This branch of a-placental mammals was cut off and diversified into a whole range of herbivorous, insectivorous and carnivorous marsupials. De Chardin calls the whole of such a flowering of a phylum a 'biota'.

Somewhere back in Cretaceous times about 100 million years ago the placental mammals began to evolve and as we go on into the most recent Tertiary age we can see their diversification into the whole mammalian biota. The dinosaurs faded away and the new major group was the warm blooded mammals. Now we are into fairly modern times and thinking of things like sabre toothed tigers and mammoths and the tiny eohippus and on through the whole gamut of evolving and refining mammals which eventually included the primates. From one line of this development came man, but the usual problem of the suppression of the peduncles makes the line of his origin fade back into the emergence of mammalia and so into the emergence of life from the water. Beyond a certain time back in history the origins of man as a species are lost. Hominid remains from several million years ago have been found in Africa. Remains of Australopithecus have been found dating back to about 2 million years ago. This precursor of modern man walked upright and used primitive tools such as chipped bones and stones. Remains of Peking man dating from about half a million years ago have been found. He is closer physiologi-

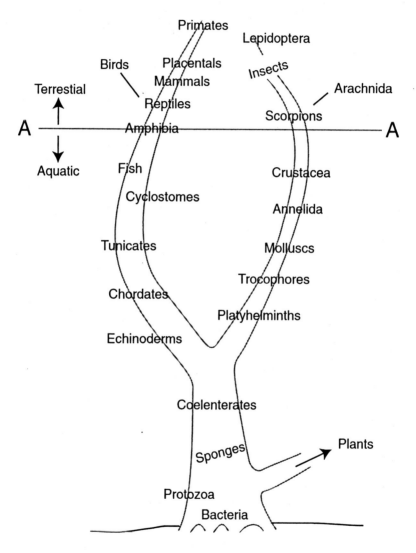

Cuenot's Tree of Life

cally to modern man than the earlier types and his brain lies midway in capacity between that of a chimpanzee and that of an advanced modern man. He is known to have used fire and to have lived in communities. There were various species of early man which were unsuccessful. The best known to us is Neanderthal man, who was widespread in Europe and the Middle East 40,000 years ago, but who was completely supplanted by *homo sapiens*, the species from which we all come.

The progress of evolution as it emerged from the primeval slime and developed into the many forms that have gone for ever and the many forms that we still see today has been mapped by a number of people including Cuenot. As can be seen from the outline sketch of his 'Tree of Life', that direction of the development of life which was to result in the plants forked off at a very early stage, right back indeed at the time when Pooh Bah's ancestors were still a protoplasmic primordial globule. As the Tree of Life grew upwards it bifurcated. One leader advanced in the direction which gave us shellfish and crabs and scorpions and spiders and insects and ants and butterflies. The other followed the path whose progress we have been looking at so far, the path that gave us fish, amphibians, reptiles including the dinosaurs from which the birds evolved, and mammals including the placental mammals from whom the primates evolved. The forms of life above the line AA live on land; below it they are aquatic. (The plant line obviously continues upwards and onwards to have forms both above and below the line, but these are not of significant interest to us in evolution as progress in capability compared with the other lines.)

Anyone who has planted and grown a tree will know that the upward growth concentrates in one leader. If for some reason or other the trunk bifurcates, there is a period of hesitancy and then one side or the other becomes the leader and the surge of growth continues on through it. The other side of the bifurcation becomes simply a branch. Similarly in the branches and smaller branches there are leaders and side shoots. This pattern can be read across to the wider picture. Back in the dim distant ages there must have been many unsuccesful types of earlier forms, just as there were unsuccessful types of early man, like the Neanderthal man whom we know to have been widespread in Europe and the Middle East about 40,000 years ago. 40,000 years is near enough to modern times for plenty of traces to be left. If we go back hundreds of millions of years then we are unlikely to find traces of the unsuccessful forms. There must have been many forms of fishes or proto-fishes. We do indeed still have one odd form of fishy life in existence today. This is the lamprey, which has only one nostril and no jaws. All the successful forms of fish apart from this which we have today developed from the eventual leader in the fish verticil, which had jaws and two nostrils. Similarly, it was the tetrapod that became the leader in the amphibian verticil. They all had a leg at each corner. This would lead us back to a particular direction of fish development which had some sort of fins at each corner and so was suitable for moving about in shallow water and over muddy tidal and estuary flats. In each group you can find the leaders of side shoots and the leaders of sub-side shoots and also, in the groups that were to produce further evolutionary stages, you can find a verticil that is a continuation of the main leader of the whole tree. Just looking at the top of our branch of the tree, the fish leader developed into the amphibians. From the amphibians there was evolution to the reptiles and a hesitation over the bifurcation there until mammals raced away as the main leader. Within the mammals, the placental mammals took over the lead and from them came the final leader, the primates, at the leading tip of which is man. If we look back down the tree we can see all the branches merging in upon each other stage by stage until differentiations are gradually lost. Even the plant forms rejoin down near the base, and we eventually reach the bottom among the bacteria.

It is a very long way back and it has all taken a very long time. Mammals began to emerge clear of the reptiles somewhere about 80 million years ago. That, however, is recent history. If we go through the three layers of reptiles, theromorphs and amphibians back to the emergence of the amphibians we are talking of something like 300 million years ago - and even that is still quite a long way up the tree. Physicists who have measured the lead content of pre-Cambrian minerals have suggested that the earliest traces of carbon in sediments date back to 1500 million years ago. If we think of the inevitable 'suppression of the peduncles' then the first living organisms may well have been considerably earlier still.

It has all been an enormously lengthy and an enormously complicated process, but one cannot fail to be struck by the ongoing development as the leader of the Tree of Life grows upwards. One sees development in complexification, development in capability, development in consciousness. de Chardin identifies two great components in this growth of complexity-consciousness. First of all there is the radial component, the complexification outwards as one goes away in time from the primordial centre. I have already touched on this to some extent. There was the complexification of the atomic structure to give the whole atomic table. There was the complexification of atoms in molecules which reached a natural limit in the mineral world. There was the other complexification in molecular development by polymerisation which took over as leader in the radial development. Finally there was the complexification of single cells into what might almost be thought of as polymer forms of cells to give more complex organisms. This is the radial or evolutionary development outwards from the first particulate beginnings. Here we see matter radiating out and progressively achieving higher forms of unity. Up to the stage at which life begins it is something which manifests itself in a compulsion to build bigger structures of greater potential. In the living world we become aware of two other great compulsions which work towards the successful overall continuation of evolution. These are the instinct of self-preservation, including improvement of the quality of life, and the instinct for reproduction of the species. The second great component is the tangential component, the component of involution. It is the energy that links and holds together the complexifying units. It is all sorts of energies such as the force of gravity, chemical bonding and so on, becoming more complex as the organisations become complex to include the forces of social organisation and mutual interdependence in increasingly multifarious and complicated forms as complexification increases. Wielding my habitual very broad brush, I will suggest that for simplicity's sake we shall regard the radial or evolutionary movement as the development and blossoming and fruition and success of forms of increasing organisation and the tangential or involutionary movement as that which links the forms together.

Somewhere in the radial development of evolution we become aware of consciousness. Where we set the starting point for the origin of consciousness depends upon how we define it, but it does not vastly matter. It would not be normal to regard a lump of rock as being conscious. Nor do I think that most people would say that a unicellular organism had consciousness in the normally accepted understanding of this term. Plants are sentient things with something at least analogous to a nervous system and some people may wish to attribute a primitive level of consciousness or pre-consciousness to them. By the time we come to fish I believe it would be normal to say that they are conscious and we can see this level of consciousness rising as we go on up the Tree of Life from there. As with the rise in complexification so with the rise in consciousness, if we go backwards down the tree we can see it decreasing until it becomes too faint and primitive to be detectable and it disappears downwards with the decrease of complexification towards the absolute beginning. What we can see if we go the other way back up the tree is that the increasing complexification eventually makes it possible to detect a consciousness which goes on rising as the complexification of the leader of the Tree of Life increases. There is a determining parameter in this rise of consciousness and it is the degree of the development of the brain, of cerebralisation. The dinosaurs are famous for being enormous in body but tiny in brain. The average mammal brain is more complexified than that of any other group of vertebrates. A closer inspection shows the degree of cerebralisation to be what one would expect for a given position on the Tree of Life. Among the mammals, for example, the biota of the placental mammals as a whole is superior to that of the marsupial mammals. Within each biota there is a gradation according to age along the biota. It has been found that the arrangement of animal forms according to their degree of cerebralisation corresponds to the classification of systematic biology. Here we can see the outward manifestation of the rise of consciousness.

There is a more difficult side to all this. It is the side that de Chardin called 'the Within of things'. He looked back in time along the rise of consciousness and declared that 'Refracted rearwards along the course of evolution, consciousness displays itself qualitatively as a spectrum of shifting shades whose lower tones are lost in the night'. This lead him to conclude that, although we could not detect it, matter must from the very outset have contained consciousness within it. That is a very hard concept to comprehend and he was rather forced into it by the fact that he was writing as a scientist, not as a metphysician or philosopher. I have no such restrictions and would like to suggest an easier way of looking at things.

Let us go back to the think-act. Let us go back to the idea that what we call 'immaterial' is just as real as what we call 'material'. It is just that we have a limited view and comprehension of things. As we have seen, actions in space-time normally require a physical agent. The whole think-act is there in the Big Bang, but to develop fully in space-time it requires the agency of matter. That happens to be the way in which Subsistent Being organised this particular think-act. Matter organised in primitive forms is only capable of primitive actions. Water can run downhill and fire can burn things, but that is about as far as it goes. With the coming of life and the rise of consciousness more and more becomes possible. What de Chardin calls 'the Within', the immaterial power of the think-act, can be progressively expressed more and more as the forms of matter develop. Increased cerebralisation means more ability to express 'the Within'. I would just like to give one concrete example to illustrate this line of thought. Put a brain, even Einstein's brain, on a pathologist's slab and it is nothing more than a collection of chemicals. It is materially just the same organ as when it was working in somebody's head, but there is a vital difference. It is inanimate, a word coming from the Latin *anima*, meaning 'wind, breath, life, spirit, mind'. An inanimate brain is a lifeless, mindless brain. One can draw the analogy with a computer. Computers do not act on their own any more than a spade digs the garden on its own. Turn the power off from a computer and it becomes nothing more than a box full of microchips and wire. The physical is clearly not the mind itself any more than a computer is its power source and programmer or a spade is the gardener. What the brain does is allow the consciousness, the power of the think-act, to act. The idea, might one say the purpose, encapsulated in the Think-act is being progressively realised by the rise of complexification that allows its increasing expression and towards which matter has been and is being directed.

This leads to the endorsement of what we more or less take for granted, that is, that placental mammals are the leader of the Tree of Life, that the primates are the leading shoot and that the anthropoids are at the tip of this leading shoot.

We have now come to the point of considering thought, but let us leave further development of that theme for later and turn now to an account of evolution that is mainly concerned with the progress of one particular group of *homo sapiens*.

THE OLD TESTAMENT – A PEOPLE IN THE EPOCH OF EVOLUTION

In the seminary in which I was educated as a lay student until I went on to the Britannia Royal Naval College, Dartmouth, there was a bookshop. Not surprisingly, a large section of it consisted of devotional books and books for religious studies and part of one shelf of this section was screened by a thick green baize curtain. The books behind this curtain were only for sale to students who had completed Sixth Form studies and were studying philosophy and theology in the final years of their priestly formation. All the books behind the green baize curtain were identical: they were the Bible.

As I said at the beginning of the book, much of the Bible consists of unexceptionable psalms and proverbs; but what I would term the bible history part is enough to make your hair curl. It is a saga of slaughter, rapine, treachery and sexual licence which might well have caused a young seminarian's eyebrows to rise, to put it mildly.

If you think I am exaggerating, let us look for a start at what happened after the Israelites came out from the wilderness. First of all it is interesting to note the size of the Israelite host. Moses took a census of all the men of twenty years old and over who were able to go to war. The total number was 601,730. If we add to that the youth and children of both sexes and the womenfolk it can be seen that the total number of the Israelites must have been somewhere around 2,000,000 people. This is much bigger than the population of the British Isles at that time, while an army of 600,000 was absolutely enormous in that day and age. It is also interesting to note that all the men who had been in the previous census when the Israelites were down in the south near Mount Sinai had died except for Caleb and Joshua. This multitude of people now marched north out of the deserts of the Sinai peninsular into Trans-Jordania.

Here I would like to make the point that the Bible has Moses and Joshua after him in receipt of constant directions from God. This constant, open line communication with God and the character of

God in the Old Testament are so peculiar to it that I intend to refer to God in the context of the Old Testament by the traditional name for that period, Yahweh.

Looked at dispassionately, it is astounding that the Israelites should spend 40 years making the journey from Egypt to Canaan. This long period of wandering was apparently a punishment for faint-heartedness when they sent scouts to spy out the Promised Land and these reported that the tribes already living there, the Amelechites, Hittites, Jebuzzites, Amorites, Canaanites, Perizzites and Hivites, were too strong for the Israelites to face them in battle. But the 40 years in the wilderness was also a time when a new generation could be bred in safety. Their daily food was provided for them in the form of manna and all they had to do was gather it up. They were safe from any enemies. They were able to breed up a new generation like a gathering swarm of locusts until the time when they came out of the wilderness with over 600,000 men of fighting age. It also made a complete break with the past. I recently heard a rabbi say on the radio that it took 40 days to get the Israelites out of Egypt and 40 years to get Egypt out of the Israelites.

Yahweh had initially promised to Abraham that he would give him the land of Canaan and the promise was repeated to Israel. It was again repeated to Moses at Mount Sinai. Yahweh was intent on giving this land to the Israelites and the poor unfortunate people living there just happened to be in the wrong place at the wrong time.

When the Israelites came out of the wilderness, Yahweh told Moses not to bother the Ammonites but to go straight on to the land of Sihon the Amorite, king of Heshbon; they were to do battle with him and take over his land; and the news of it would make everyone else terrified of them. Moses then sent messengers saying that they only wanted passage through the land on the road and that they would buy any food or water that they needed. Sihon replied that he did not believe in Santa Claus and turned out his army. Upon this, the Israelites attacked him, captured all his cities and killed every man, woman and child. Then they went on to the land of Og, king of Bashan.

There Yahweh said to Moses, "Do not fear him for I have given him and all his people and his land into your hands and you shall do to him the same as you did to Sihon the king of the Amorites". The Israelites duly killed every man, woman and child and destroyed the king's sixty cities. In both cases they looted the cities before destroying them and took all the herds off with them. These territories, which are to the east of the Dead Sea and to the east of the River Jordan were given to the tribes of Reuben, Gad and Manasseh. The only thing that makes this campaign different from those of Genghis Khan and Attila the Hun is that the Israelites intended to settle on the land afterwards. There is no suggestion of provocation or evil-doing by Sihon or Og. They were just in the way and so their subjects were extirpated, men, women and children; their goods were looted; and their cities were destroyed. All this was done at the direction of Yahweh.

Then we come to the crossing of the Jordan and the conquest of Canaan, the Promised Land, itself. The book of Joshua starts with Yahweh saying to Joshua, the new leader, "Moses my servant is dead; now therefore arise, go forth over the Jordan to this land that I am giving to you, to the people of Israel. Every place that the sole of your foot will tread upon I have given to you, as I promised to Moses. From the wilderness and this Lebanon as far as the Great River, the River Euphrates, to all the land of the Hitites to the Great Sea towards the going down of the sun shall be your territory. No man shall be able to stand before you all the days of your life; as I was with Moses, so I shall be with you; I will not fail you or forsake you." Yahweh then held back the waters of the River Jordan just north of the Dead Sea so that the Israelites could all walk across to Jericho. Yahweh then told Joshua that the army was to march once round Jericho each day for six days; on the seventh day it was to march round seven times and blow the trumpets and shout and the walls would fall down. Thereupon the Israelites slaughtered the inhabitants and burned the city. Then the Israelites went west to Ai. Yahweh dictated their exact tactics to them and as a result they took the city and slaughtered all the 12,000 inhabitants, male and female. The poor unfortunate king was hanged on a tree. Then the kings of Jerusalem and five other city states took the field against Israel, realising that they were probably going to be next in line for slaughter; and slaughtered most of them duly were. The five kings were taken during the pursuit and thrown into a cave. When the Israelites had all come back from the chase, Joshua had the five kings taken out of the cave, killed them personally in front of the people and had their bodies hung up on trees until evening. Then Joshua marched against the northern kings, who had formed a defensive alliance under the king of Hazor, a town to the north of the Sea of Gallilee. The Israelites defeated the northern army, looted and destroyed the cities, drove off the cattle and killed all the inhabitants. According to the Book of Joshua, this was the direct wish of Yahweh, "for it was the Lord's doing to harden their hearts that they should come out against Israel in battle, in order that they should be utterly destroyed, and receive no mercy but be exterminated, as the Lord commanded Moses".

There is a list of 31 kings who were dealt with in this way during the conquest of Canaan. To this must be added the slaughter and destruction on the east side of the Jordan. There were 60 cities in the kingdom of Og alone. It is recorded that 12,000 people were killed at the destruction of the city of Ai. It therefore seems likely that in this initial conquest of Trans-Jordan and Canaan somewhere between 1,000,000 and 2,000,000 men, women and children were slaughtered for no other reason than that they were occupying the land wanted by the Israelites. Some of this killing was done completely in cold blood. Numbers 31 records what happened when the Israelites attacked the Midianites. They killed all the men and burned the cities, then returned to their camp on the east side of the Jordan with the Midianite women and children and herds and the rest of the plunder. Moses was angry that they had let the women and children live. He gave orders that they should kill all the male children and adult women (thus ensuring that any unborn males would also be killed), sparing only the young, virgin girls for themselves. As the spoils of war were to be divided between the army who had gone out to fight and those who had remained behind, everything was counted up, and it is recorded that there were 32,000 virgin girls. If we assume that the numbers of juvenile males and numbers of adult females were each similar, this means that some 60,000 women and boys were butchered in cold blood outside the Israelite camp. Those who carried out the massacre had to stay outside the camp for a week so that they could lose the reek of blood and the stench of death. This terrible act was carried out on the express orders of Moses, who was the long-established link with Yahweh, from whom he received regular instructions. Nowadays in prayers we use expressions such as 'Most merciful and loving God'. I hope I am beginning to make it clear that there is a dichotomy between the Old and New Testaments. I will suggest a reason for it in due course.

Another well known tale of slaughter is one where the slaughtering was done by Yahweh himself. When Pharoah would not let Moses and the Israelites leave Egypt, the land was visited by a succession of plagues. First of all the river turned into blood. Then there was a plague of frogs, followed by a plague of lice, followed by a plague of flies. Then there was a plague that killed the cattle and oxen and asses and camels and sheep, while those of the Israelites were left unharmed. In the next plague the Egyptians were covered with sores. Then there were dreadful hailstorms and lightning. This was followed by a plague of locusts which ate everything in sight. Pharoah appeared ready to let the Israelites go, but as soon as the locusts went away he changed his mind. The next plague ws a plague of darkness for three days. Once again Pharoah appeared ready to agree but again he change his mind when the plague was lifted. So we come to the final plague, the killing of all the firstborn throughout Egypt. This was the first Passover, a name originating in the fact that the Israelites were instructed to put lamb's blood on their doorposts and Yahweh 'passed over' these houses without killing the firstborn inside. After this the Egyptians could not be rid of the Israelites quickly enough.

46

After they had gone, Pharoah changed his mind again and set out with all his army to bring them back again. We are told that Yahweh 'went before them [the Israelites] by day in a pillar of cloud to lead them along the way, and by night in a pillar of fire to give them light, so that they might travel by day and by night; the pillar of cloud by day and the pillar of fire by night did not depart from before the people'. The Egyptians caught up with the Israelites by the shore of the Red Sea. Yahweh said to Moses, "Tell the people of Israel to go forward. Lift up your rod and stretch out your hand over the sea and divide it, that the people of Israel may go on dry ground through the sea. And I will harden the hearts of the Egyptians so tht they shall go in after them, I will get glory over Pharoah and all his host, his chariots and his horsemen, and the Egyptians shall know that I am the Lord." Meanwhile the pillar had been between the Egyptians and the Israelites, keeping them apart. The Israelites duly walked across on the dry sea bed, but when the Egyptians went in after them in pursuit Yahweh said to Moses, "Stretch out your hand over the sea, that the water may come back upon the Egyptians, upon their chariots and upon their horsemen". And so the Egyptian army was drowned by the direct intervention of Yahweh, while the Israelites safely reached the other shore.

Treachery was a frequent feature of this story, too. We come upon a good example very early on when Isaac's wife Rebecca schemed to have Esau replaced by her second son, Jacob, as the one who would receive Isaac's blessing. The tale is well known. Rebecca dressed Jacob in Esau's clothes and covered his neck and hands with goat skins because Esau was a hairy man and Jacob was not. Rebecca cooked the kids to provide the meal that Isaac had asked for as the last meal before he died and sent the disguised Jacob in to him with the food. As Isaac was too old to see clearly, he asked which son it was. Jacob boldly lied and said that he was Esau, then invited his father to eat and give him his blessing. Isaac was not completely convinced, so he made Jacob go up to him so that he could feel him. When he felt the fur of the goat skins he said, "The voice is Jacob's voice but the hands are the hands of Esau." Then he formally blessed him and made him his heir, saying that he should be lord over his brothers. When Esau found out and complained about what had happened, Isaac did not reverse his decision but ordered Esau to serve his brother. He left his blessing with the more resourceful and able of the brothers, the one who would best further the interests of the family. Far from being punished for his treachery, the leadership of Jacob - or Israel, as he later became - was endorsed by Yahweh and he became the founder of the Israelite people.

Sexual activity in the Old Testament was an a magnificent scale, at times even heroic or gargantuan. The pop song says that Solomon – the very same Solomon who built the temple for Yahweh in Jerusalem – had a thousand wives. 1 Kings says that he actually had seven hundred wives of royal status and the other three hundred were concubines. However, the end result is much the same! Gideon, who lead the Israelites when 100,000 Midianites were slaughtered, had 70 sons. As we are told in Judges 9 'for he had many wives'.

Another notable example is the founder of the Israelite nation, Israel himself. You will remember that he was originally called Jacob and with his mother's guidance had cheated his elder brother Esau out of his inheritance. It was thought politic that he should go away and stay with his uncle Laban. While there, he married both of Laban's daughters, his cousins Leah and Rachel. He really wanted to marry Rachel, the younger daughter, but Laban cunningly substituted Leah for her on the wedding night. (More treachery). Nothing daunted, Jacob married Rachel as well. Jacob fathered four sons on Leah, sons who were to be the first four of the founding fathers of the tribes of Israel. These were Reuben, Simeon, Levi and Judah. Rachel meanwhile appeared to be barren. This made her worry about the security of her position in Jacob's favour, so she went to him and urged him to take her servant Bilhah as his concubine. Rachel said that if Bilhah had a child by this union she would herself squat under Bilhah at the birth so that the baby would be born into her lap and she would take it as her own. Jacob duly widened his efforts to include Bilhah and on her he fathered the next two founders of the tribes of Israel, Dan and Napthali. Leah had not had any more sons during this time and now it was her turn to feel that her position was slipping, especially as she was the plain one and Jacob had not wanted to marry her in the first place. So she in her turn took her maid Zilpah to Jacob and urged him to take her as his concubine. She also said that she would squat under Zilpah at the birth so that the baby would be born on to her lap and she would take it as her son. Jacob widened his efforts once again and his next two sons were born from Zilpah. These were two more of the founding fathers, Gad and Asher. Jacob was evidently still trying his best with all four of them because Leah then produced sons nine and ten, Issachar and Zebulon. Finally, Rachel herself conceived and had a son called Joseph. Then she conceived again and this time she died giving birth to the last son, Benjamin. So we have the start of the Israelite people. Jacob underwent one final testing, which is described as wrestling with an angel, and at the end of that he was told to change his name to Israel. His sons became the founders of the twelve tribes of Israel and their fathering had been spread out among the two sisters to whom Jacob was married and their two maidservants who were his concubines. Here was another tale to make a young seminarian's eyebrows shoot up.

****

So what are we to make of this brutal, primitive and earthy tale? I would like to suggest that it is a story governed by the exigencies of evolution, a story where the interests of the radial force are supreme. The Israelites are known as the Chosen People, chosen by Yahweh for his own special care and attention. They seem to have been something of an unrewarding choice, to say the least, as they put up altars to Baal or golden calves or Moloch just about every time the bell struck. Presumably the competition was even less promising. The Israelites may have been fickle and hard hearted, but they did seem to have large amounts of get-up-and-go. The Jews through the ages, hated and reviled though they may often have been, have always been a people of outstanding capability. From learning to finance to music, from Einstein to Rothschild to Hammerstein, they are still a people of enormous talents. Look indeed at Joseph in Egypt. He arrived there as a slave, having been sold by his brothers (another charming story of malice and treachery!). From that inauspicious beginning he rose to become Pharoah's right hand man and ruler of all Egypt for him. He invited his brothers and their families to join him and they became so numerous and prosperous that the Egyptians

50

eventually enslaved them for fear that they would take over the country. We are told that when they left Egypt 430 years later there were 600,000 men, besides the women and children. This is patently a people of enormous capability.

If Yahweh was looking for a leader, a leading shoot for the human branch of the Tree of Life the obvious place to select one was in the Middle East. This was the power house of evolution 4,000 or more years ago. We are told that Yahweh chose Abraham. Yahweh told Abraham to go away from his family group in Haran and go on with his immediate family into Canaan, present day Israel. He said "Go from your country and your kindred and your father's house to the land that I will show you. And I will make you a great nation, and I will bless you, and make your name great so that you will be a blessing." After wandering down as far as Egypt, Abraham settled in Canaan. In passing it is interesting to note the small scale of things in these pastoral days of following herds. When Abraham went to rescue his nephew Lot from other local chieftains his total force was 318 men. Some time after this Yahweh made his promise to Abraham, the Covenant, saying, "Behold, my covenant is with you, and you shall be the father of a multitude of nations. No longer shall your name be Abram but Abraham, for I have made you the father of a multitude of nations. I will make you exceedingly fruitful; and I will make nations of you, and kings shall come forth from you. And I shall establish my covenant between me and you and your descendants after you throughout their generations for an everlasting covenant, to be God to you and to your descendants after you. And I will give to you, and to your descendants after you, the land of your sojournings, all the land of Canaan, for an everlasting posession; and I will be their God." A similar promise was repeated later when Abraham showed that he was willing to offer his only son Isaac in sacrifice. This Isaac was the father of Jacob, the Isaac who passed on the blessing of Yahweh to Jacob and his successors. This is why the Israelites referred to themselves as the Chosen People. From this

51

time onwards we have the record of the constant direction and guidance given by Yahweh.

The Old Testament spans the time from the Big Bang right up to the era of the Persian kings who invaded Greece in the 4th century BC. We have seen earlier how evolution progressed until at last man appeared on the scene. Very primitive man would scarcely have been a suitable subject for divine guidance. We may assume that by the time of Abraham man's mental and social progress was sufficiently advanced to make it worthwhile. Yet it was still very early and primitive days, with penny numbers of itinerant herdsmen living in tents. By the time the Israelites left Egypt after their 400 year stay there they were a nation of some 2,000,000 people and their civilisation had marched on apace. By the end of the story we are into Greek times and early Roman times.

Quite a lot of what went on in the Old Testament – like Moses ordering 60,000 women and children to be butchered in cold blood - seems quite terrible now to us who bring a man to court for smacking a naughty child with a slipper. How could Yahweh have condoned such things and in some cases apparently done similar things himself? In suggesting an answer to this and making the beginnings of a suggested answer to the dichotomy between the Old and New Testaments I would like to turn first of all to a book by Plato. It is a dialogue called the Euthyphro and happens to have made a particularly deep impression on me because it is the only one that I was obliged to read in the original Greek at school. Euthyphro is coming back from the law courts where he has put his father on trial for impiety when he comes across Socrates, himself soon to be condemned to death for corrupting the young. Socrates sees that this has possibilities and says words to the effect of, "Ahah! If you have put your father on trial for impiety you are just the person to help me by telling me what goodness is. So please tell me, what is goodness?" Euthyphro replies that goodness is what the gods love. Well, he was on a hiding to nothing after that because Socrates was quick to point out that the Greek gods disagreed and quarrelled about nearly everything. The discussion ran on, with Euthyphro making various attempts to improve on his definition. He never managed to satisfy Socrates, yet his instinct seems to have been sound. His problem was that there were lots of gods. If there is only one God then he seems to me to have got it right. Evil is discordant and there can be no discord in perfect Subsistent Being. He is goodness by definition. So we must surely ask ourselves what was pleasing to Subsistent Being on this earth in Old Testament times? What was the purpose, what was the aim of the progress of the think-act we are part of in biblical times? I have already suggested that the main thrust was radial growth, evolution. We therefore take as a rough definition that what was good was what furthered the progress of evolution. Furthermore, in comparative terms, what was more good was what furthered the group evolution of the Chosen People. If we look at things from this viewpoint then the pattern of this violent and vigorous story begins to fall into place.

****

Our two strongest instincts are apparently that for self-preservation and that for procreation. As I have already mentioned, in my book self-preservation is more than avoiding being killed by predators or starvation. It is the instinct to preserve ourselves as well as we can. We not only want to avoid starvation; we want to have plenty to eat. We not only want to have a roof over our heads; we want a comfortable place to live. We want food that is plentiful and delicious to eat. We want clothing that is comfortable and stylish and good to look at. We want possessions for our comfort and interest and indeed to display the success of our self-preservation and give us prestige which will further enhance our quality of life. I include all this under the instinct for self-preservation. The instinct for procreation is complementary to this. If we all succeed in preserving ourselves to good effect but do not procreate then evolution stops with us.

There is a further extension to the workings of self-preservation and procreation. This is good order in the society in which we live so that this society does not itself become a threat to the furtherance of the said evolution by self-preservation and procreation. Let us look first of all at the Ten Commandments in this light. They were given to Moses at a watershed in the history of the Israelites. Symbolically - and Yahweh seems often to have driven home his points by symbolism – the Ten Commandments were given to Moses on Mount Sinai after the Israelites had trekked south down the east side of the Gulf of Suez, away from Egypt. The Covenant had been made with Abraham; the Israelites had gone into Egypt and increased enormously in numbers during the 400 years they spent there; and now they had left Egypt behind. After they left Mount Sinai they began a new epoch in their history where they went north and moved into the Promised Land. During the 400 years that the people had been growing from a small tribe to a host 2,000,000 strong they had been living in a society structured by another people, the Egyptians. Now they were moving to take possession of a land where they would be setting up their own society on an enormously increased scale and they needed a framework of rules to ensure that the society which they did set up was not hostile to their success. In the first three Commandments Yahweh first of all makes clear his own pre-eminent position:

'You shall have no other gods before me. You shall not make for yourself a graven image or any likeness of anything that is in heaven above or in the earth beneath or that is in the water under the earth; you shall not bow down to them or serve them; I the Lord your God am a jealous God, visiting the iniquity of the fathers upon the children to the third and fourth generation of those who hate me, but showing steadfast love to thousands of those who love me and keep my Commandments.

You shall not take the name of the Lord your God in vain; for the Lord will not hold him guiltless who takes his name in vain.

Remember the Sabbath Day, to keep it holy. Six days you shall labour, and do all your work; but the Sabbath Day is a sabbath to the Lord your God; in it you shall do no work, you, or your son, or your daughter, or your manservant, or your maidservant, or your cattle, or the sojourner who is within your gates.'

These three Commandments, given first of all, make it clear that first and foremost and most importantly the Israelites must remember the source of all their favours and give due deference to Yahweh. Expressed in terms applicable from further down the Tree of Life, every stable pack has to recognise a pack leader. The rest of the Commandments are a thumbnail sketch of how to construct an equitable society.

'Honour your father and your mother, that your days may be long in the land which the Lord your God gives you.'

This rule is the cornerstone for stability and good order in the immediate family, the unit from which the whole society is made up. A stable and orderly family is the bedrock of a stable and orderly society.

'You shall not kill.'

This is the most basic rule for relations in groups and between groups in a society, relations between individuals and between families.

'You shall not commit adultery.'
'You shall not steal.'

The 'eternal triangle' is one of the most common and persistent causes of friction, feud, mayhem and murder in society. It always has been and it continues to be so even today. Extra-marital affairs have caused everything from killings to broken homes to broken hearts. Our sexual urge is second only to our urge for self-preservation and marriage does not mean that it is therefore only aroused by our lawful partner. Adultery might be looked upon as a form of stealing and I suppose that by and large it is the one which arouses the strongest rage in the wronged party. But all other stealing is a similarly destabilising thing, likely to lead to quarrels and retribution.

'You shall not bear false witness against your neighbour.'

This is something that is tailor-made for causing trouble in a society.

'You shall not covet your neighbour's house; you shall not covet your neighbour's wife, or his manservant, or his maidservant, or his ox, or his ass, or anything that is your neighbour's.'

If Hector had heeded this, Troy might still be standing. Trying to obtain something that belongs to someone else by scheme and subterfuge is something that is directly contrary to the harmonious life of a group of people living together.

So we can see that, after Yahweh has set out the deference that is to be given to him, he first of all identifies the most important stabilising factor in society, the family, and then identifies the most common and serious causes of friction and forbids them. The Ten Commandments were the framework for the continued successful evolution of the Israelite nation.

There is another commandment that was not spelled out by Yahweh and written on tablets of stone like the others but which is implicit in them and which can be seen to be enforced. It might be stated as, 'Thou shalt not take thy football home'. If the think-act is going to develop then we have to take part in it. In earlier ages the problem simply did not arise. The dinosaurs did not stop to consider – they could not stop to consider – whether or not they wanted to go on eating and mating. The sabre toothed tiger was incapable of pausing to decide whether or not to go on humting. This all changed with the advent of reflective consciousness in man. Man is able to stop and consider whether or not he wants to do something. Man has the capability to say, "I think this is a silly game and I am not playing in it. I'm taking my football home." Deliberate flouting of the progress of the think-act was something not to be tolerated. Yahweh spelled out very clearly that his supremacy was to be acknowledged and respected. The Israelites were being given the unique privilege of his direct support but in return they had first of all to acknowledge his lordship and secondly to do what was required of them.

While Moses was on Mount Sinai receiving the Ten Commandments the people became bored with waiting and made a golden calf to worship as their new God. For this they were visited by a plague. Quite soon after the departure from Egypt they came to the southern edge of the Promised Land and sent scouts ahead to spy it out. Yahweh had promised very clearly to Moses on Mount Sinai that he would give the land over to the Israelites, "Behold, I will make a promise. I will do wonders for all your people such as have not been done anywhere in any nation. And all your people shall see the work of the Lord, for it is a wonderful thing that I will do. I will drive out before you the Amorites, the Canaanites, the Hittites, the Perizzites, the Hevites and the Jebuzzites. Not only must you make no agreement with the people living in the land to which you are going, you shall destroy their altars and break their images. And you shall worship no other god than the Lord. You must keep all my commandments and worship me according to my laws." However, when the spies came back they gave a negative report. They said that it was indeed a land flowing with milk and honey, but the people living there lived in walled cities and were too numerous and powerful to be conquered. "All the people we saw were men of great height. We saw they are giants, sons of Arak who are descended from giants. We looked like grasshoppers by the side of them." Then the Isralites threatened to stone Moses for leading them into such a situation.

Yahweh's response was uncompromising. The Israelites were condemned to stay in the wilderness for a further forty years and during that time the whole generation that had come out of Egypt would die, with the sole exceptions of Joshua and Caleb, because they had argued in favour of going ahead with the invasion of Canaan.'Thou shalt not take thy football home' indeed!

Another case in point of revolt at an individual level is that of Onan. Judah ordered his son Onan to lie with Tamar, the widow of his brother Er, so that she could have children. Onan could not refuse in public. He had intercourse with Tamar but in the privacy of their tent he, as sailors are wont to say, 'got off at Fratton'. He withdrew at the last moment, doubtless feeling sure that Tamar either would not know or, if she did realise, would not wish to face all the trouble of accusing him to Judah and trying to prove it. But he was struck down on the spot for this rebellion. It has long been popularly put about that Onan was struck down for masturbating and Onanism is indeed given in dictionaries as a synonym for masturbation; but there is no suggestion of this in the bible narrative. This quite specifically says that he had intercourse with his brother's widow and the description is one of *coitus interruptus*. Ahah, thought Onan, you can take a horse to water but I am not playing this game. Zap! Onan is another case of being smitten for taking his football home.

The classic story epitomising all this is that of Lucifer. We are told that Lucifer was the brightest of all the angels until one day he said, "I will not serve". He was not willing to continue playing in a game run by somebody else. He was taking his football home. Zap! He was zotted for disobedience caused by pride.

'Thou shalt not take thy football home'. This may be an unwritten commandment, but it is one that underlies the whole of the rest and one whose breaking invites the direst penalties.

Another idea that has to be mooted in the context of comprehending Old Testament history is that many of the things which we look on as important – and indeed they loom very large in the lives of those directly affected – are neutral in terms of evolution. This is so of life and death *per se*. Each contingent being is born, makes whatever contribution it does to the onward progress of the Tree of Life and then dies. Most of us are gardeners to some extent or other. We see the roses on our rose bushes appear as buds, develop into their full fragrant beauty, linger on overblown and fading, then fall, leaving the hip containing the fertilised seeds for the next generation of rose bushes. Roses are in point of fact rather a special case because we never expect to use the seeds as such in our own gardens ourselves. Some horticulturalist raises the seedlings, grafts them on to a vigorous wild rootstock and then sells us the bushes ready for planting. Perhaps I should have illustrated my idea with something more homely like the pansy or marigold; but the rose is such a beautiful flower that it is by far the most evocative. These beautiful flowers meet many forms of fate. Some are attacked by insects; some are blighted by the weather; some may be stunted by drought and wither as unopened buds; some carry out a complete and flawless life cycle. In evolutionary terms the only important thing is that they should bloom in sufficient numbers to ensure the continuation of blooms in the next generation. Looking at space-time from the detached viewpoint of Subsistent Being, there is probably little difference between the cycle of a human being and the cycle of a rose. We are all going to be born, grow, hopefully reproduce and then die. In evolutionary terms it matters little whether an individual dies in infancy, is killed by accident, is carried off early by disease or lives a full life span. We must also put down a marker here for the principle of natural selection. The evolution of living things has progressed from the outset through the success of the healthiest and most competent at the expense of the sickly, the weak and the incompetent. This was true within a given species and it is also true of the relationship between species. It was always weakest – or least well adapted to the condi-

59

tions - to the wall. Weak calves could not keep up with the herd, straggled and were taken by wolves. The very unintellectual dinosaurs disappeared from the face of the earth, except for those that had turned themselves into birds. The early waves of humans were one further step in the same ongoing process. The only essential thing was that sufficient human beings should follow the instincts for self-preservation and procreation to such good effect that the leader of the Tree of Life continued to take evolution onwards. And if one particular section of the human race was chosen to be the leader in evolution then the only important thing was that the self-preservation and procreation of this tribe should continue successfully. I would suggest that bible history makes very good coherent sense if looked at from this viewpoint.

If we take the greatest good in Old Testament terms as being the continued successful evolution of the Israelite people, then we can see why Yahweh encourages or endorses or condones the sort of conduct calculated to merge a young seminarian's eyebrows with his hairline. Trying to accept this idea of goodness is traumatic because it is so foreign to the morality which has been our own background. This radial, evolutionary goodness is that of the survival of the fittest, of nature red of tooth and claw, of weakest to the wall. It is the ethos which made Schopenhauer declare that the stuff of the universe was energy, but it was malevolent. However, if one takes goodness from the Big Bang to the end of the Old Testament as being that which furthers evolution, the radial development, the growth of the Tree of Life, then it was good that the poor old dinosaurs were superceded by the mammals or Neanderthal Man by *Homo Sapiens*.

As a final thought in this consideration of the Old Testament I would like to come back to the down-to-earth simplicity of the times and the lack of sophistication of Yahweh's contact with the Israelites. During the flight from Egypt, the wanderings in the wilderness and the conquest of the Promised Land the presence of Yahweh was generally physically apparent to the Israelites by way of a cloud or fire. These were very simple symbols and very much in keeping with those for whom they were intended, a great concourse of people trudging through the desert sands carrying their possessions. Everything was at a simple, even primitive, level. This applies also to Yahweh's portrayal of himself. He tends to portray himself as being more or less the same sort of thing as the other gods on offer but more powerful. For example, we have Yahweh saying to Moses, "Go in to Pharoah and say to him, 'Thus says the Lord, the god of the Hebrews'". When Yahweh told Moses that he would divide the waters of the Red Sea so that the Israelites could walk across in safety, he went on, "And I will harden the hearts of the Egyptians so that they shall go in after them, and I will get glory over Pharoah and all his host, his chariots and his horsemen. The Egyptians shall know that I am the Lord when I have gotten glory over Pharoah, his chariots and his horsemen." This sort of thing is typical of the level at which the activity of the Yahweh of the Old Testament is pitched. It is at a vastly lower level than that of all-transcending Subsistent Being, but it is simple stuff for a simple age. The activities of Yahweh in slaughtering the Egyptians on the night of the Passover and in the Red Sea and in encompassing the slaughter of hundreds of thousands of the people of Trans-Jordania and Canaan would probably be viewed as genocide by a UN court in this day and age. But it was not this day and age: it was the age of the radial force, the age of evolution. The highest level of goodness was that which benefitted evolution, and supreme among it was that which benefitted the evolution of the Israelite people.

THE NEW EPOCH OF INVOLUTION –
THE ADVENT OF CHRIST

By far and away the most universally recognised major division of time is into BC and AD. A Moslem may privately date things from the year of Mahomet's flight to Mecca; or the Japanese may privately date his affairs from the enthronement of the mythical first human Emperor, Jimmu, in 660 BC. However, the dates that they are constrained to use in an open international environment conform to BC and AD. The coming of Christ can therefore be called 'epoch-making' in the most brutally literal sense of the word. I would like in due course to dwell on who Christ was and why he came at all, but first of all I would like to make some suggestions as to why he came when he did. In many years of wearing out my trousers on pews and organ stools this is a subject I can never recollect hearing addressed from the pulpit in any detail.

If you are going to have an epoch-making effect upon the history of mankind, then the infrastructure has got to be suitable. To use an absurd illustration, it would be no use talking metaphysics to a bunch of Stone Age cave dwellers who had just learned to chip flakes off flints. Their language would not contain the necessary words even to make a start. Their lives, their thoughts and their language would be concentrated on daily needs for hunting and gathering, for shelter from the elements, for rudimentary social organisation. It would be difficult, to put it mildly, to take them through the first few chapters of this book. If we move on several centuries to the time of the historical characters in the early Old Testament narrative, they were still very simple people. They were nomadic herdsmen who followed their flocks and lived in tents. Further sophistication came to the Israelites during their long sojourn among the Egyptian civilisation. This was more complex in structure, a large scale kingdom with cities and an administrative infrastructure. When the Israelites returned to the Promised Land they too established a kingdom with a capital city containing Solomon's magnificent temple. They became civilised in the literal sense of being a kingdom based on city dwellers and it is always the case that the establishment of cities makes possible the emergence of a class of scholars and thinkers whose existence is incompatible with a primitive, nomadic society. The same sort of thing was of course happening elsewhere in the Eastern Mediterranean and Middle East region. I have already mentioned Egypt. Another long-established cradle of civilisation was the Fertile Crescent, the area around Mesopotamia – an old title not much used nowadays that means 'between the two rivers', the Tigris and the Euphrates. There had been civilisation there since the time of Ur of the Chaldees and there were famous empires of Medes and Persians and Assyrians and Babylonians. In its heyday, Babylon took more than a day to walk across. Human society was becoming more complex and with this complexity came added dimensions of thought and language. Then, about four centuries before Christ there came the rise of the Greek city states. It was in the leading Greek city state of Athens that there arose groups of men intent upon addressing fundamental issues of philosophy. Everybody has heard of Socrates, Plato and Aristotle. An eminent present day Professor of Philosophy has observed that all that philosophy has done since that time has been to put a gloss on the philosophy of Aristotle. This may or may not be true (it is most certainly not true of the far-ranging and innovative ideas of de Chardin), but thought and language were carried forward by the Greeks to a stage where abstract concepts could readily be discussed and absorbed.

With the flowering of the work of the Greek philosophers it could be said that mankind had reached a mental plane ready for epoch-making information of a philosophical nature. The other thing necessary was that this information could be disseminated. It would have been no good for Christ to have preached his message in the rainforests of Brasil. The message would have remained there. Various kingdoms and empires ebbed and flowed in the relatively civilised Near and Middle East, but they were localised and mutually inimical. For a suitable vehicle it was necessary to await the rise of the

Roman Empire. This was large, stable, homogeneous and efficiently administered. It encompassed the whole of the Mediterranean littoral, the southern half of Europe and a considerable part of the Middle East. It was an empire on an unparalleled and unprecedented scale. By the time that Constantine made Christianity the official religion of the Roman Empire at the beginning of the 4th century it was well ordered and coherent and it contained within it the economic and academic springs of the West.

Thus when Christ came there was a high enough mental level to take his message on board and there was a vehicle ready for its dissemination so large that the message would never disappear. At last and for the first time the evolutionary epoch had reached such a stage that it ready to greet a new epoch.

Who was this person through whose agency the new epoch arrived, whose coming was to divide the calendar of the whole world into BC and AD? Before starting to think about why Christ came and what the new epoch was that he introduced, it is nothing more than natural to pause to consider who he was. I shall work toward that on the basis of a syllogism. The major is this:

'If a man claims to be God and God supports that man his claim must be true.'

This stems straight from the attributes of God and God as Subsistent Being which were discussed in the early part of the book and on that basis it is simply a plain statement of fact. You may recall that I said then that much of that part was a series of BGOs, but that they were very useful building blocks. The major of this syllogism is built directly on them and with them. In its turn it may be considered to be another BGO, but this in its turn becomes a very useful building block for further progress.

The minor of the syllogism parallels the form of the major and I would like to illustrate its two parts in turn.

'But Jesus Christ did claim to be God'.

The Gospels are studded with claims by Christ that he was God. I shall of course not attempt to list them all but simply concentrate on a few very clear instances, particularly ones where the meaning was evident to his hearers. Having said that, I feel that I cannot start without including the little story of the cure of the paralytic in Capharnaum.(Mt9)(Lk5). Luke tells us that there were so many people that the poor man had to be let down on his bed through a hole in the roof to ask to be cured. However, Christ did not immediately cure him but told him his sins were forgiven. The scribes and Pharisees began to mutter at this, saying, "Who is this that speaks blasphemies? Who can forgive sins but God only?" Christ threw it straight back at them, "Which is easier to say, 'Your sins are forgiven you', or to say, 'Rise and walk'? But that you may know that the Son of Man has authority on earth to forgive sins" – he said to the paralytic – "I say to you, rise, take up your bed and go home". When he asked his disciples whom they thought he was (Mt16), Peter answered, "You are the Christ, the son of the living God,". Christ, far from denying this, answered, "Blessed are you, Simon-bar-Jonah! for flesh and blood has not revealed this to you but my Father who is in heaven." Then there is the famous passage at the conclusion of John 8 where Christ says, "Your father Abraham rejoiced that he was to see my day; he saw it and was glad." The passage continues, 'The Jews then said to him,"You are not yet fifty years old, and have you seen Abraham?" Jesus said to them, "Truly, truly I say to you, before Abraham was, I am".' This is an absolutely blunt claim to be God because of that final present tense. The name Yahweh is the representation of God's definition of himself to Moses as "I am who am". (Ex3) In other words, Abraham lived in time but he, Christ, lived in eternity. The Jews took his meaning and tried to stone him for blasphemy. A little later on at the feast of Dedication some of the Jews gathered round him in the Portico of Solomon in the temple and asked him, "If you are the Christ, tell us plainly." Christ's answer concluded with the words, "I and the Father are one". Once again the Jews made ready to stone him and, when he asked him why, they replied, "It is not for the good work that we stone you but for blasphemy; because you, being a man, make yourself God." There was no doubt at all about the Jews's understanding that Christ was claiming to be God. Again, when under exmination by the High Priest (Mt26), Caiaphas asked him straight out, "I put you on oath by the living God to tell us if you are the Christ, the son of God". "You've said it," replied Christ, "but I tell you hereafter you will see the Son of Man seated at the right hand of Power and coming on the clouds of heaven." Caiaphas got the message. He tore his robes and said, "He has uttered blasphemy. Why do we still need witnesses? You have now heard his blasphemies". The final example I would like to cite does not indeed contain a claim by Christ to be God; it is just an acknowledgement of that claim by the Jews. Pilate was evidently puzzled at the vehemence with which the Jews pressed him to have Christ executed. Eventually he felt constrained to point out, "I find no crime in him". The Jews answered him, "We have a law, and by that law he ought to die, because he has made himself the son of God".

So we see that Christ did claim to be God. Now let us move on to the second half of the minor:

'And God supported him'.

We can start by going back to the paralytic let down through the roof at Capharnaum. When Christ told the man to take up his bed and go home as a validation of his claim to be able to forgive sins, the paralytic duly did it. Christ's public life is studded with the support of divine power made manifest in the working of miracles. These were of three main kinds. Firstly, there were those worked on men, i.e. cures of diseases (leprosy, paralysis, dropsy, etc), cures of the blind and deaf and dumb, and three cases of raising the dead to life. One of these last was the case of Lazarus, who had been sealed up in his tomb for four days. When Christ asked for the stone to be rolled back from the entrance to the tomb, Martha demurred because she was sure that there would be an unpleasant smell of decomposition by this time. The second sort of miracles were those worked on spiritual beings i.e. casting out devils (seven cases were reported). The third sort were those worked on inanimate nature (changing water into wine, stilling the tempest, twice multiplying loaves and fishes, walking on water, etc). Having already found it reasonable to accept the Gospels as historical narratives, it is reasonable to accept that these events happened. It does also seem reasonable to accept that the effects produced were miraculous and could only be attributable to a supernatural cause. It is really straining credibility to say that the sick people were comforted and felt better and the credulous Apostles wrongly thought that they were wholly cured. These cures were worked in public so that even the incredulous Jews had to admit them. Going back to the case of Lazurus (Jn12), when Martha demurred Christ said, "Did I not tell you that if you believed you would see the glory of God?" 'So they took away the stone and Jesus lifted up his eyes and said, "Father, I thank thee that thou hast heard me. I knew that thou hearest me always and I have said this on account of the people standing by, that they may believe that thou did send me." When he had said this he cried with a loud voice, "Lazurus, come out". The dead man came out, his hands and feet bound with bandages and his face wrapped with a cloth. Jesus said to them, "Unbind him and let him go." The Jews who had seen this were so impressed that the Pharisees became worried. 'The chief priests and Pharisees gathered the Council and said, "What are we to do? This man performs many signs. If we let him go on thus, everyone will believe in him,". Nor can the lesions of leprosy be cured by hypnotism or suggestion. Furthermore, all cases of leprosy cures had to be examined and certified by the priests in accordance with the rules laid down in the Law. Nor is faith-healing the answer. Faith-healers hold that if the sufferer is persuaded that he can be cured then the natural power

67

of the body moves to cure itself. However, the dead are not capable of acts of faith.

It therefore seems to me to be far more reasonable to accept the fact that Christ worked miracles than to reject it. Where does that take us? The whole point of these miracles was to support his claim to be God. When John the Baptist sent his disciples to Christ to ask him if he was the promised Messiah he answered, "Go and relate to John what you have heard and seen. The blind see, the lame walk, the lepers are cleansed, the deaf hear and the dead are raised up, and the poor have good news preached to them". When the Jews criticised him for healing on the Sabbath (Jn5) he replied, "For the work that the Father has granted me to accomplish, these very works which I am doing, bear me witness that the Father has sent me". He worked his miracles in defence of his teaching that he had been sent by the Father, to show that he had God's support.

The other great demonstration of divine support is of course the Resurrection. Once again, he said very plainly that he would rise from the dead and the Jews just as clearly understood his meaning. When the scribes and Pharisees asked for a sign he answered, "An evil and adulterous generation seeks for a sign; but no sign shall be given to it except for the sign of the prophet Jonah. For as Jonah was three days and three nights in the belly of the whale, so will the Son of Man be three days and three nights in the heart of the earth". After the Transfiguration (Mt17) he said to Peter, James and John, "Tell the vision to no man until the Son of Man is risen from the dead". He said to the Apostles as they were going up to Jerusalem for the final Passover (Lk19), "Behold, we are going up to Jerusalem, and evrything that was written of the Son of Man by the prophets will be accomplished. For he will be delivered to the Gentiles, he will be mocked and shamefully treated and spat upon; they will scourge him and kill him, and on the third dy he will rise". The prophecy was explicit and it was clerạly understood, for (Mt27) the chief priests and the Pharisees gathered before Pilate and said, "Sir, we remember how the imposter said, while he was still alive, 'After three days I

68

will rise again'. Therefore order the sepulchre to be made secure until the third day, lest his disciples go and steal him away, and tell the people, 'He has risen from the dead', and the last fraud will be worse than the first". 'Pilate said to them, "You have a guard of soldiers; go, make it as secure as you can". So they went and made the sepulchre secure by sealing the stone and setting a guard.'

We can be sure that, having succeeded in having Christ crucified, the Jews made sure that he duly died on the cross. But there is an even more reliable witness. A Roman centurion was given the job of making sure that all three of the crucified men were dead. The soldiers broke the legs of the other two men; but when they came to Christ and found that he was already dead, one of the soldiers drove his spear through the body just to make sure. When Joseph of Arimathea came to ask for the corpse for burial (Mk16), Pilate wondered if he were already dead. He therefore summoned the centurion, who duly confirmed that this was so. It seems to me that any deception, hallucination or trance hypotheses are utterly unreasonable non-starters. If the scribes and Pharisees and Roman centurion were all satisfied that Christ was dead, then it is immeasurably more reasonable to take it that he was dead.

The Gospels tell the story of the empty tomb found by the women on the Sunday morning. The stone was rolled away; the linen cloths were wrapped up inside the sepulchre; and an angel announced his resurrection. The Gospels go on to recount nine different appearances of Christ; to Magdalen in the garden, to the women as they ran back to tell the Apostles, to Peter, to the two disciples on the way to Emmaus, to the Apostles in the upper room when Thomas was absent, to the Apostles in the upper room when Thomas was present, to the seven Apostles by the Lake of Tiberias, to the Apostles in Galilee when they were given their commission to teach, and again when they were led out and Christ ascended from their sight. Paul also gives a full account of the death, burial and resurrection in his letter to the Corinthians and refers to other appearances not recorded by the Evangelists, i.e. to five hundred people at once, to James, and to

Paul himself. Apart from the general reasonableness of accepting the Gospels as a historical narrative, as they were accepted by the people of those days and has already been discussed, perhaps the most cogent argument is a negative one. The Apostles would never have got away with such a story unless it had been true and, furthermore, they would not have had the stomach to try and get away with it. They were shattered, crushed, demoralised. They had nothing to gain by deception. Nor were they credulous. Thomas expressed it with great clarity (Jn21), "Unless I see in his hands the print of the nails, and place my finger in the mark of the nails and place my hand in his side, I will not believe". The Apostles had been huddled in an upper room for fear of the Jews, but after seeing the risen Christ they went out to proclaim the Resurrection. Furthermore, they worked miracles in the name of the risen Christ. Luke says (Acts6) that among the early converts 'a great multitude of the priests obeyed the faith'. The priestly class had condemned Christ because they rejected his claims and miracles. That many of them were converted now showed that they had the evidence of his Resurrection; he had given the sign they had asked for. For them it meant breaking with their class and livelihood, yet conscience obliged them to do so. They must have been absolutely convinced either from the Apostles teaching or miracles or by the reconsideration of the evidence, but we may be sure that they examined well the evidence of his Resurrection and were converted because they were convinced that he had indeed risen. As Paul said (1Cor15), Paul who preached the risen Christ, 'If Christ has not been raised, your faith is futile'. Futile? AD and BC!

There is one more point I would like to make about the Resurrection. There is no suggestion anywhere that Christ simply came out of the tomb, got dressed and went on with a normal daily life in the way that Lazarus did. It was something very different. The two disciples who walked with him along the road to Emmaus did not know who he was. The penny suddenly dropped when he broke bread for them at supper that night. Well, perhaps they had never got very near him before; perhaps they had been two of the Charlie

70

Browns of this world who always get stuck at the back of the crowd. This was certainly not so in the case of Mary Magdalen, but the first time she met Christ after the Resurrection she took him for the gardener. We are told that the Apostles were keeping a low profile in an upper room with the doors bolted for fear of the Jews when Christ came and stood among them. The Resurrection was clearly not just a resumption of normal daily life. With the incarnation of Christ, Subsistent Being took on the body and nature of a man and physically entered into this particular think-act. By this I mean that he entered in a continuous, tangible way into our dimensions, the dimensions of space-time, and became an actor in this think-act. This is something completely different from the burning bush that appeared to be on fire but was never consumed or the gentle wind that blew on Isiah. Nobody would suggest that God entered the think-act as a bush or a wind. They were no more than indicators. But Christ was different. He was demonstrably a man who was born, grew up and was killed. God had entered into the dimensions of this think-act in our nature. This is not something that we can apprehend fully because of our division into material and immaterial. Perhaps the best analogy for us is that of a dream. In our dreams all the actions takes place immaterially and we seem to be taking part in them. Even though it is all in the mind – or what I shall subsequently refer to as the no-osphere – our adventures seem utterly real and are unlimited in scope. It may indeed perhaps be fair to say that they are real happenings in the no-osphere! In our dreams we can eat and drink, paint the house, make love, go sailing, play the trombone, be chased by a bull or do anything else at all that we might do in the physical life. Shakespeare made some uncannily perspicacious philosopohical comments and one of them was 'We are such things as dreams are made of'. Perhaps the nearest analogy that we can make is that we are a dream of God and God does not have our problem of the division into material and immaterial. I would like to push the analogy a little further, remembering that it is no more than an analogy and is not a direct parallel. We can do anything in a dream, but if we are about to be

71

killed or if we apparently are killed then we wake up. We remove ourselves from that dimension. In an analogous way, when Christ was killed God removed himself from continuous physical participation in our dimensions. I would suggest that this is what the Resurrection was. It was not a coming back to life but a complete removal of all that was embodied in Christ materially and immaterially from permanent presence in space-time. God was and is of course able to manifest himself again to us at any time under any form, but I suggest that the Resurrection was not a coming back to life but a complete withdrawal of the incarnation of God as an ordinary human being from our dimensions.

Before moving on to the third and final part of this section to discuss what was the message brought by Christ this seems to be a good juncture to pause and ponder for a moment on another matter concerning God which has caused much rancour and division over the years. I refer to the matter of unity and trinity. The opening words of a hymn on the subject of the Trinity by Cardinal Newman in the last century are 'Firmly I believe and truly God is three and God is one'. Such an idea is so impossible to explain that it has been dubbed a mystery and booted firmly into touch. Yet it may not be quite as difficult as it seems. It all really depends on how you look at it. In the modern vernacular of those who serve you in a shop with the words, "There you go" (which is really not any more idiotic than the statement of the obvious normally used previously, "Here you are"), it all depends on where you are coming from.

Cristian doctrine states (Penny Red), 'There are three persons in God: God the Father, God the Son and God the Holy Ghost'. The extent of the problem or lack of it depends on what you mean by 'person'. Words inevitably come to have associations and the word 'person' immediately brings to our minds three separate people like, say, Charlie Chaplin, Mother Theresa and Nelson Mandela. Now these three people all have separate qualities and abilities and characters. They have different physical characteristics: Mother Theresa is a woman and the other two are men; Nelson Mandela is black and the other two are white. They also have completely separate and distinct reflective consciousnesses.Their memories, understandings and wills are quite separate. Their thought processes are quite separate.

Now three persons in one God cannot be like Charlie Chaplin, Mother Theresa and Nelson Mandela. From all that was written at the beginning of the book about the attributes of God there is no room for denial that God is one. It was shown that God is Subsistent Being and that he is simple and infinite. 'Simple' meant that he could not be made up of parts and is incapable of division. It was pointed out that if God were to be made up of parts then these parts are infinite or finite; if they are finite, then a number of finites can never make an infinite; nor can the parts be infinite because it is impossible by definition to have more than one infinite. One infinite could only be distinguishable from the other by the presence of a perfection in one that was lacking in the other, but by definition an infinite has the fulness of being or perfection and cannot lack a perfection. There is only room for one infinite, so God is one. That is a brief restatement of points already made in the chapter on the attributes of God. There is one simple, infinite God who is Subsistent Being and is not capable of being divided into parts.

How then does the Trinity fit in? There cannot be three separate beings like three separate people because there is only room for one infinite being who is perfect i.e complete and lacking in nothing. Words are slippery things. The mad philosopher Wittgenstein became quite fascinated by them.He came to think that the structure of language had to structure the reality that it represented and that unless this was so we could not talk meaningfully about the world in language. Conversely, as we know that meaningful discourse is possible, he felt that we could find out about the structure of the world by analysing the structure of language. In a later work he put forward the idea that the meaning of a word was its use in the language. That seems to me to be approaching the dictum of the Humpty Dumpty in 'Alice in Wonderland' who said, "Words mean exactly what I want them to mean, nothing more and nothing less". That may be so in Wonderland, but here in our everyday world words have associations which it is in actual fact virtually impossible to take away from them.

It may be helpful to speculate on how the concept of the Trinity arose. Unlike other nations who worshipped a multiplicity of gods, the Jews worshipped one God alone, Yahweh. They needed to be able to distinguish between Yahweh and the divine man who lived among them. Peter put it in a nutshell when he said, "Thou art the Christ, the son of the living God". Christ was a man who had been born by the power of God; he was the incarnation of God walking among them as a human; it was thus natural and apposite to call him the Son of God. Then finally there was the need to be able to able to refer to God as apparent in the tongues of fire which rested over the heads of the disciples on Whit Sunday. The 'Holy Ghost' was the name that the early Christians gave to the spirit and power of God which was left with them after the physical, human presence of Christ had been withdrawn. The idea of three in one and one in three grew out of these concepts.

It has become normal to refer to the 'three persons' of the Trinity. Unfortunately the word 'person' has strong associations for us. If we just think in general of three persons, we think of three distinct human beings, like our Charlie Chaplin, Mother Theresa and Nelson Mandela. 'Person' is associated in our minds with a separate entity. Thus even though we know that God is simple and indivisible we still depict the three persons of the Trinity separately, God the Father as an old man with a long white beard, God the Son as a young man and God the Holy Ghost as a dove. We do this in spite of the fact that we know that logically they cannot be separate beings. Interestingly enough, there is a strong similarity between the tongues of fire of the New Testament and the burning bush of the Old Testament. However, the Jews before Christ made no attempt to divide Yahweh because he appeared through a burning bush – nor indeed because he appeared as a pillar of cloud or fire during the escape from Egypt. It is also interesting to note that Christ, far from pointing to divisions in God, was at some pains to emphasise the oneness of God, saying things like, "He who has seen me has seen the Father", or "I and the Father are one"

Perhaps it would be more helpful to look at what we are really thinking about in each case. Persona was originally the mask worn by an actor to show the character he was. It was an indication of the part he was playing, of his activity at the time, of his role. Are we not really referring to some role or quality of simple, infinite and indivisible Subsistent Being? It is customary to think of God the Father as the creator, the source of force, power and action; to think of God the Son as a visible manifestation of this; and to think of God the Holy Ghost as the mental power of God. These are aspects of three fundamental facets of space-time with which we are familiar: firstly, energy; secondly, the manifestation and fixation of energy as light, heat, matter etc.; and, thirdly, reflective consciousness. 'Persons' is an unhappy choice of word. It has the implicit meaning of 'beings' for us. Yet we know that logically there is not room for more than one indivisible Subsistent Being. As a professional translator of Japanese documents with many years experience I am very well aware of how difficult it is to find exact correspondence in meaning. The Latin tres personae does not have the same meaning as that which we associate with the English 'three persons'. It would perhaps be more helpful to use words like 'aspect' or 'facet' or 'function' and view the Trinity as the manifestation of the three aspects of Subsistent Being that are the fundamental pillars of this his creation of space-time – energy, manifestation of energy and consciousness. Might we perhaps best describe the Trinity as our present vision of Subsistent Being as refracted to us through the dimensions of our space-time?

Let us now move forward to the third and final main part of this section dealing with the coming of Christ. We have looked at why Christ came when he did and we have looked at who Christ was. Now let us look at why Christ came.

Prior to Vatican II, the explanation given for the coming of Christ was expounded with great frequency, certainty and precision. It was the doctrine of the Atonement. The argument ran as follows. Adam and Eve were being tested as the representatives of mankind. They were specially privileged and aided by having four freedoms, viz, from death, ignorance, sorrow and concupiscence. When they yielded to temptation at the Fall, they lost these four freedoms for the whole of the future human race and life on earth became, as Hobbes so pithily put it, 'nasty, brutish and short'. Now the only person of sufficiently high estate to make full restitution to God for the affront offerred to him was God himself. Therefore God became incarnate, that is, he took on the nature of man, having a body and soul like ours, and by sacrificing his life on the cross he made full restitution to God on behalf of mankind for the sin committed by their representatives Adam and Eve. The whole story of the Garden of Eden was taken as absolutely factual, however unreasonable it appeared to regard it as being so.

The story of the Garden of Eden was not a straightforward one, to say the least. Some parts of it seemed to be allegorical. What was this 'tree of knowledge'? Eve is traditionally pictured biting into an apple, but it was obviously not an apple tree. What did this expression 'tree of knowledge' stand for? And what was the serpent? It was unreasonable to think that it was a talking snake. Even without any wider background knowledge the story of the Garden of Eden appeared to be allegorical. It was very hard to be certain of exactly what the whole story symbolised. However, if one accepted that Adam and Eve were being tested as the representatives of the human race and that they failed on behalf of the whole human race, then the doctrine of the Atonement proceeded with an inescapable logic. The whole doctrine of the Atonement was not a very mentally satisfying one and I remember that it produced a certain amount of muttering among my classmates. The thing that was hardest to swallow was that an almighty, infinite, omniscient God should have so bodged things up and so painted himself into a corner that the only way he could extricate himself and restore his self-respect was to become incarnate as a man and be savagely done to death. We felt that however sound the logic (assuming that one accepted the literal truth of the story of Adam and Eve) there had to be something more than this.

I sometimes used to wonder as to the authorship of Genesis. I supposed it was probably Moses. Eventually I had some spare time to browse in a library in America, which has a strong Jewish academic tradition, and found a great deal of writing on the subject of Genesis. The author was not Moses, as I had supposed up until then. Different parts of Genesis were written down in 3 different periods by three authors or sets of authors, the Yahwist (c.950BC), Eloist (c.800BC) and Priestly (c.550BC, after the Babylonian Captivity). Where did the story come from? I also found the answer to that.

In actual fact, Genesis up to the point where it becomes the story of Abraham and the Chosen People does not tell a unique story. It is based on the common folklore and mythology of the Fertile Crescent, the lands around the Tigris and Euphrates rivers and swinging round through present day Syria and Lebanon to the Mediterranean. Inscriptions in wedge shaped cuneiform script were discovereed as early as the 17th century, but it was not until the 1840s that an Englishman, Henry Rawlinson, made real progress in deciphering cuneiform. In the years that followed, archeological expeditions discovered many more panels and tablets inscribed with cuneifrom and brought them back to England. Henry Smith, another Englishman and a protege of Rawlinson, catalogued the finds and published translations. Two of the biggest finds were the Enuma Elish or Creation Epic (1,000 lines) and the Epic of Gilgamesh (3,000 lines). There are accounts of the separation of earth and sky, the moon and stars, creation of man,

'Let me put blood together and make bones, too.
Let me set up primeval man. Man shall be his name.'
and the great tower of Babylon, the ziggurat for the god Marduk
    to rest at,
'Create Babylon whose construction you requested !
Let its mud bricks be moulded, build high the shrine!'

77

In the Epic of Gilgamesh, the hero is distressed by the death of his friend Enkidu and sets off to see Utnapishtim, the only man to be granted immortality because he survived the Flood after being instructed in detail to build an ark by the god Ea.

'Dismantle your house, build a boat.
Leave posessions, search out living things,
Reject chattels and save lives!
Put aboard the seed of all living things, into the boat.'
Utnapishtim duly did so.
'I put on board the boat all my kith and kin.
I put on board cattle from open country, wild beasts from open
      country..'

As the waters receded, Utnapishtim sent out a dove, then a swallow, both of which came back. Finally he sent out a raven, which did not return. The gods then granted Utnapishtim immortality because he had survived the Flood. When Gilgamesh leaves, Utnapishtim gives him as a parting gift a plant of rejuvenation. However, one day a serpent stole the plant as Gilgamesh bathed. It appears that the serpent was connected with the idea of immortality and the tree of life in the Fertile Crescent because it was thought to have the power of rejuventation on account of the fact that it could slough off its old skin.

The Epic of Gilgamesh and another tale about Enki and Nimbursag, the Great Mother Goddess, both speak of Dilmun, the garden of the gods, where sickness and old age were unknown. Enki was cursed by Nimbursag because he ate eight special plants that she was growing in Dilmun. Another interesting thing is the old name for the Mesopotamian plain, which was irrigated and became famous for its fertility. In Sumerian this plain was called Edin (the same as Eden if one allows for the vagaries of transliteration and spelling),the plain of Sumer in the north and Akkad in the south (later Assyria and Babylonia respectively). Flooding was of course common in Mesopotamia.

So we find in these Mesopotamian myths a great number of the components incorporated into the early part of Genesis. It seems evident that the earliest part of the Bible is not unique but is to a greater or lesser extent a re-editing of myths and legends already widely current in the Fertile Crescent, since the cuneiform tablets considerably pre-date even the Jahwist parts of Genesis. Tablets of the Epic of Gilgamesh, for example, date from the early part of the 2nd millenium BC. What is more, archeological excavations have discoverd even earlier evidence of the existence of these tales. In a 3rd millenium BC Akkadian seal illustrating the Epic of Gilgamesh there are a man (Gilgamesh) in a boat holding the tree of life and another man who was perhaps Ur-shanabi, the boatman. The notable difference between the Bible and other accounts is that it is monotheistic and God operates from outside creation.

We must also take into account the work of Darwin and all the anthropologists, palaeontologists and archeologists. When the authors of Genesis wrote down their own version of the old Mesopotamian myths they followed their lead in having Adam suddenly created as man by God blowing on dust and Eve created by God fashioning her from one of Adam's ribs. We cannot but conclude that in this they were factually incorrect. They were writing primitive rubbish.

So as a result of scholarship we came to know in the latter part of the 19th century that the story of Adam and Eve and the Garden of Eden is just a melange of Mesopotamian myths. If this is so, it follows there was no such thing as 'the Fall'. Is it not amazing that many years later we were required to accept a fundamental and crucial line of thought which hangs entirely on taking the story of Adam and Eve as undiluted, literal fact? Were Christian scholars so blinkered that they never ventured to read the research of non-Christian scholars? Or did fear of being burnt at the stake as a heretic deter inquisitiveness? Or could it possibly be that it was deemed unthinkable to rock the boat after so many centuries

One final thought that I would like to offer about the story of Adam and Eve is this. We are told that Adam and Eve became aware that they were naked and made clothing out of leaves. Now apes have no such consciousness. Could it be that the story of Adam and Eve is intended to conclude the initial account of evolution by allegorically describing the advent of reflective consciousness with the coming of man?

If God had wanted to become incarnate to make restitution to himself or indeed for any other reason he could have done it at any time. Yet there was this lengthy period from the time of Adam to the coming of Christ when the status of mankind was, to say the least, uncertain in its relationship with God. Mankind was left in a kind of limbo evolving for several thousand years. I feel I have made what I think to be a reasonable suggestion that Christ came when he did because only then were the human mental level and the human organisational level adequate to receive a new direction, a new message.

What was this message of Christ that has wrought such a transformation? Why did he come? He did not go about saying that he had come to restore the balance of justice upset by the wrong done by Adam. His message was one of love, co-operation, consideration for others. This is a frequently recurring theme in the Gospels. We have become thoroughly acclimatised to it by having it preached at us for nigh on two thousand years. There seem to be more sermons on charity than on anything else (or all the rest put together? – or perhaps it just feels like it!). The idea has become embodied in the Christian ethic and through it in the ethic of the secular state. We no longer experience a sensation of shock, horror, bewilderment and disbelief on being told to turn the other cheek and do good to those that hate us. Yet what an earth-shattering point of view this must have been when the message was first preached in those days when evolutionary good was king, in those Old Testament days of an eye for an eye and a tooth for a tooth in that land founded on aggression and the slaughter of men, women and children, the land of the hard-hearted people of the hard God Yahweh.

Yet this is the theme to which Christ returns frequently and at length. There are many well known examples in the Gospels and I shall cite only a few of them, beginning with the very well known Sermon on the Mount.(Mt5). It was soon after Christ had begun going about preaching and curing the sick and crowds had begun to follow him about. He went up on to a hillside – I suppose this was so that everyone could see him – and then began to talk to them in a most unusual way. The record of his remarks starts off with what are known as the Eight Beatitudes. These are so well known that everybody will have heard of at least some of them, but they were epoch-making stuff in that day and age. Call to mind if you will the cultural environment depicted in the section on the Old Testament in this book and, bearing that in mind, just read over the Eight Beatitudes again.

'Blessed are the poor in spirit, for theirs is the kingdom of heaven.
Blessed are those who mourn, for they shall be comforted.
Blessed are the meek, for they shall inherit the earth.
Blessed are those who hunger and thirst for righteousness, for they shall be satisfied.
Blessed are the merciful, for they shall obtain mercy.
Blessed are the pure in heart, for they shall see God.
Blessed are the peacemakers, for they shall be called the sons of God.
Blessed are those who are persecuted for righteousness' sake, for theirs is the kingdom of heaven.'

This was trail-blazing stuff, a new direction, but there was a lot more to come, such things as these.

'You have heard that it was said to the men of old, 'You shall not kill; and whoever kills shall be liable to the judgement'. But I

81

say to you that anyone who is angry with his brother shall be liable to the judgement, whoever insults his brother shall be liable to the council, and whoever says, 'You fool!' shall be liable to Hell fire.'

Again,

'You have heard that it was said, 'An eye for an eye and a tooth for a tooth'. But I say to you, 'Do not resist one who is evil. But if anyone strikes you on the right cheek turn to him the other also; and if anyone would sue you and take your coat, let him have your cloak as well; and if anyone forces you to go one mile with him, go with him two miles.'

And again,

'You have heard that it was said, 'You shall love your neighbour and hate your enemy'. But I say to you, 'Love your enemies and pray for those that persecute you, so that you may be sons of your Father, who is in heaven; for he make his sun rise on the evil and on the good, and sends rain on the just and on the unjust.'

We are told that when Christ had finished his discourse the crowds were astonished at his teaching, for he taught as one who had authority.

There are also many examples of Christ preaching and practising forgiveness. There was (Jn8) the case of the woman caught in the act of adultery. The Pharisees tried to catch Christ out by asking him whether they should stone her as the law of Moses commanded. Christ simply said, "Let he who is without sin among you be the first to throw a stone at her". And then he ignored them, apparently engrossed in something he was writing with his finger in the dust, until they all finally melted away. Christ then looked up at he woman standing by and said, "Woman, where are they? Has no-one condemned you?"

She said, "No-one, Lord." And Christ said, "Neither do I condemn you; go, and do not sin again".

Another well known example was the case of Mary Magdalen. This little cameo had particular force and point because it happened in the house of a Pharisee where Christ had been invited to dinner. Mary Magdalen was a notorious sinner and the Pharisees were quite aghast when Christ did not recoil as she bathed his feet in ointment and washed them with her tears and dried them with her hair. They thought he was not much of a prophet if he did not know the sort of woman that was touching him. Christ then told his host that he had something to say to him. "A certain creditor had two debtors; one owed five hundred denarii and the other fifty. When they could not pay he forgave them both. Now which of them will love him more?" His host answered, "The one, I suppose, to whom he forgave more". Christ told him that he was quite right and went on to point out to him that when he entered the house he had been given no water to wash his feet and no kiss of welcome and no oil to anoint his head, but the women had washed his feet with her tears and kissed them and anointed his feet with ointment. He went on, "Therefore I tell you her sins, which are many, are forgiven for she has loved much".

There were many, many occasions on which Christ preached forgiveness and mercy. Forgiveness, mercy and love. Another very well known example of his preaching on these themes is that of the Good Samaritan. Indeed the story is so well known that it does not even need to be repeated here. What I would just like to pick out is the conversation with the lawyer before the start of the story. We are told that a lawyer stood up to put him to the test and said, "Master, what shall I do to inherit eternal life?" Christ asked him what the Law said about it, "What is written in t he Law? How do you read it?" The lawyer answered, "You shall love the Lord your God with all your heart and with all your soul and with all your strength and with all your mind; and your neighbour as yourself". Christ answered, "You have answered right; do this and you will live".

Duirng the Sermon on the Mount Christ had been at pains to make it clear that he had not come to abolish the Law. He said he had come not to abolish it but to fulfil it. There was still the need to give due deference to God and to have a society that did not disintegrate through internal discord. But there is this new theme, this positive theme that is so much further advanced than the 'Thou shalt nots' of the Commandments. The commandments of forgiveness, mercy and love are 'Thou shalt' commandments. 'You shall love the Lord your God with all your heart and with all your soul and with all your strength and with all your mind; and your neighbour as yourself'. In his final words to the disciples before going out to be arrested and killed, Christ said, "A new commandment I give to you, that you love one another; even as I have loved you, that you also love one another. By this all men shall know that you are my disciples, if you have love one for another".

So this is the epoch-making message that came to divide history into BC and AD: love God and love your fellow men. The point is hammered home by Paul in his first letter to the Corinthians in a passage which could hardly be surpassed for eloquence and includes the following,

'If I speak in the tongues of men and of angels and have not love, I am a noisy gong or a clanging cymbal. And if I have prophetic powers and understand all mysteries and all knowledge and if I have all faith so as to move mountains, but have not love, I am nothing. If I give away all I have and if I deliver my body to be burned, but have not love, I gain nothing.

Love is patient and kind; love is not jealous or boastful; it is not arrogant or rude. Love does not insist on its own way, it is not irritable or resentful; it does not rejoice at wrong, but rejoices in the right. Love bears all things, believes all things, hopes all things, endures all things.'

The particular passage ends,

'So there abide faith, hope and love, these three; but the greatest of these is love'.

This may not seem at first sight to be epoch-making stuff, but it proves upon examination to be nothing more or less than the signal to change from concentration on evolution to concentration of involution. It signalled the change from the primacy of the radial to the primacy of the tangential. Radial development is that of complexification. It is the development where we start with basic particles which combined into atoms and then molecules; where organic molecules, essentially carbon compounds, polymerised and so were able to reach an enormous size and complexity; where some of them 'came alive' and evolved into the cell, the building block of living creatures; and where we then have the well known succession of evolution through fish and amphibians to mammals and so on eventually to man. After the arrival of man upon the scene his experience and mental powers developed over the millennia until the stage was set for the arrival of Christ. This is the radial path of evolution. That is not to say that at the same time there was no involution. The tangential energy of involution is the one working to link things together, to arrange things. We can see its effects from very early on in social structure. We can see it in groups still existing today from various levels of the Tree of Life. We have shoals of fish and flocks of birds. We have birds pairing and working together to raise a brood of chicks. We have a number of pairs working alongside each other doing the same thing in a rookery. We have prides of lions and herds of gazelle. We also noted how there was symbiosis among an organisation including herbivores, insectivores and carnivores. Finally with man we reach a social involution which had developed to quite a complex level of civilisation by the time of Christ. Things were already moving in an involutionary direction and the time was ripe for a redirection, but we must remember that in historical terms the period since the advent of man has been very short. Except for a period at the end so short that it would not register historically, the BC era was the era of radial development, the era of the rise of complexity, the era of the rise of consciousness.

Now the prime commandment was to love. I say the prime commandment advisedly because Christ was at pains to make it clear that the other commandments stood. The greatness of God must still be acknowledged and society still had to be stable and not self-destructive. However, love is an involutionary force which draws together. What is love? I would like to suggest that it is the non-material expression of attraction. It is the non-material force that parallels physical forces of attraction which we know and have been able to quantify in expressions such as $(m_1 + m_2)/d^2$. The effects of love can be physical: we may pat a dog or cuddle a baby or give up our place in the lifeboat because of this force of attraction. Love is characterised by wanting to be as close as possible to the thing loved. Yet although the effects of love may often find physical expression, it still seems fair to me to say that love itself is essentially a non-material attraction. So love and involution now bring us to consideration of some non-material aspects of this think-act.

But there is just one final thought I would like to float before moving on. If there was no Fall and therefore no need to make restitution for the whole human race, why did Christ die on the cross? Could it be that instead of dying on the cross because He had to, He died on the cross voluntarily, a willing human scapegoat to demonstrate love, His love of humanity, in action as a beacon blazing out the new message of love and involution?

IMMATERIAL FIELDS

If you meet a friend whom you have not seen for six months or more, there is not normally any particular problem in recognising him. His face looks just the same - unless he has had plastic surgery or grown a beard. But it is not the same face at all. It is indeed a completely different face. The cells which are our building blocks are constantly being renewed with fresh material from the food we eat. All the protein in the body is renewed at least once in six months. So if we meet a friend after a lapse of time of six months or more his whole face has been renewed even though it looks just the same. Why should it look the same? Why do not the cells in his nose renew themselves in a shape like that of Cyrano de Bergerac or in a hooked nose or a Roman nose or a snub nose or even a nose that is all on one side? For an introduction to this area I turn to the work of Harold Saxton Burr.

Now I must say at the outset that this man is no New Age nutter. Dr Burr was for 43 years a member of the faculty of Yale University School of Medicine, teaching anatomy and neuro-anatomy. He ultimately became the E.K. Hunt Emeritus Professor of Anatomy at this university. His portrait hangs in the Yale University Medical Library. During his time as an academic at Yale he published no less than 93 scientific papers and after his retirement he drew some of his salient thoughts together into a fascinating book (Blueprint for Immortality).

If you support a piece of paper over a magnet and scatter iron filings on it, they will arrange themselves into a pattern, the pattern of the 'lines of force' of the field of the magnet. If you throw them away and use fresh filings, the result is exactly the same. Most of us will have carried out this little experiment at school. In a similar way there is a force field around the human body, although it is much more complicated than that around a single magnet. In a similar way to that in which the magnet always makes the iron filings take up the same pattern, this 'field of life' or L-field acts as the matrix or mould for our body, preserving the form and the organisation of the cells no matter how often they are renewed. Much of Burr's work was directed towards these L-fields. His research showed that all forms of life from slime to man were ordered and controlled by electrodynamic fields that could be measured and mapped accurately. Like all the forces in physics they are part of the complete structure of the cosmos, mutually influencing and being influenced. As in all fields of physics, the L-fields play a part in organising and directing and they reveal man to be an integral part of a universe which, far from being a chaos, can be observed to be directed and ordered throughout.

There is a good reason why Harold Burr was one of the first into this field of research. When he began his experiments there were no instruments generally available that could measure the L-fields without disturbing them. The L-fields are a manifestation of potential differences, very very small differences, and using them to make a current flow disturbs and drains the field. When Burr embarked on this work in the 1930s, the instruments that measured electrical properties of living things were operated by the electrical output of the system. This method was a complete non-starter for things as delicate as the L-fields. A possible solution was shown by a man called Lund, who used an electrometer. For the benefit of those who, like myself, have long left school or have a limited scientific background I should perhaps mention that an electrometer is a type of voltmeter in which potential difference is measured by the mechanical forces between electrically charged bodies, the repulsion of two similarly charged bodies being read directly off a calibrated scale. Another pointer given by Lund was in avoiding direct contact with protoplasm by metal electrodes, which lead to unpredictable and unreliable measurements. Lund made indirect contact with the protoplasm with zinc sulphate electrodes via the medium of water or cell sap.

The instrument that was to make the measurement of L-fields accurate and reliable was the vacuum-tube voltmeter. These are commercially available today but in the 1930s Burr had to spend years devising and perfecting his own system of instrumentation. Commercial models which were sufficiently sensitive and stable gradually became available and ultimately he was able to settle on the Hewlett Packard DC vacuum tube voltmeter Model 412A for measuring L-fields. He used a physiological salt solution as a bridge between the protoplasm and electrodes and found this always the best for high precision work; but he also found that for long term experiments involving slightly larger potential differences of the order of millivolts it was acceptable and much simpler to use an inert salt paste as the bridge.

Measurement of L-fields produced some fascinating information. One subject for experimentation was the frog's egg. Different voltage gradients across different axes of the egg were measured and the axis of the largest voltage gradient was marked. It was found that as the egg developed the frog's nervous system always developed along the axis of the highest voltage gradient. Here was an indication of the L-field acting as a matrix to shape the morphology of the system. Other experiments were made using the embryo of the salamander. Measurements began with the unfertilised egg and it was found that even the unfertilised egg possessed an axis for development of the nervous system which was maintained after fertilisation. The electrometric correlate of the design of the living embryo could be recorded during growth and was like a pattern imposing direction on it. It was also discovered that the voltage gradient could be discovered out to as far as $1\,^1/_2$ mm away from the embryo and that although the field of the embryo radiated through the medium of its liquid environment the field properties of the embryo did not short out in the liquid, as would happen in the case of the voltage gradient of a battery. It was also found that when the embryo was rotated the field rotated with it, producing a sine wave output to the detecting electrodes.

Electrostatic fields only exist where there are charges and, conversely, wherever there are charges there are fields. These are fundamental properties of the chemical components which go to make up living matter, but the fields in living matter become enormously com-

89

plex. Burr stated his theory in the following terms, 'The pattern or organisation of any biological system is established by a complex electrodynamic field which is in part determined by its atomic physio-chemical components and which in part determines the behaviour and orientation of those components. This field is electrical in the physical sense and by its properties relates the entities of the biological system in a characteristic pattern and is itself, in part, a result of the existence of those entities. It determines and is determined by the components. It must maintain pattern in the midst of a physio-chemical flux. Therefore it must regulate and control living things. It must be the mechanism, the outcome of whose activity is wholeness, organisation and continuity.'

As a neurologist Burr had established that a very important factor in the organisation of the nervous system was the existence of differential growth rates within the wall of the neural tube. Furthermore, there was a relationship between the direction of growth of the end of the differentiating nerve fibres and centres of proliferation. It has also been shown that growth is linked to bio-electrical phenomena.

Another interesting illumination of the interaction between the electrodynamic field and the physio-chemical components emerged during experiments on sweet corn kernels. Pure strains were used as a control and the difference in L-fields between these and hybrid strains were observed. When measurements were taken of the mean potential between the ends of the corn kernel it was found that there were striking differences between the single gene mutant and the parent stock. This leads to the conclusion that there is a close relationship between genetic constitution and the electrical pattern and that the medium through which chromosomes impart design to protoplasm is very likely that of an electrodynamic field.

L-fields are also affected by changes in condition of the living being. Many experiments were carried out over a long period of time on human beings. The electrodes were put into two cups containing salt solution and the subject then put the index finger of the left hand into one cup and that of the right hand into the other. It was found that there was a voltage gradient between the left finger and the right finger that was reasonably constant for a given human being but which varied between different humans from about 2 to 10 millivolts. The voltage was more or less constant, that is, except that female voltage gradients showed a sharp rise from time to time for a period of 24 hours. As these rises occurred roughly in the middle of the menstrual cycle it seemed likely that they might be associated with ovulation. Tests were first of all made on female rabbits, which ovulate nine hours after stimulation of the cervix. The surface of the ovary was kept under observation by microscope and it was found that the moment of rupture of a follicle and release of the egg was accompanied by a sharp change in the voltage gradient on the electrical recorder. When the opportunity came to carry out similar observations on a human subject during an abdominal operation, this confirmed that what had been supposed was indeed the case. When the potential difference between the central abdominal wall and the wall of the vagina rose markedly, the laparotomy was performed and the recently ruptured follicle was noted at the ovary. Here then we have a change in voltage gradient associated with fundamental biological activity. Conversely, it was discovered that state of mind can affect the state of the field. There can be physical manifestations of psychosomatic illness. Strong emotion can produce a voltage rise of as much as 20 millivolts. As Burr drily observes, heartbreak may one day be measurable in millivolts.

There are many potential medical applications of L-fields, such as checking the internal progress of wound healing or detecting malignant growths from distortion of the field. One wonders also about possible connections between acupuncture and focusses of intersection of L-fields. One wonders if Indian fakirs are able to produce effects by mental concentration on such intersections. Some healers do indeed seem to be able to sense the field around a patient and detect problem areas through the irregularity or abnormality of the field in the area. Can they then exert the force of their own field to restore normality? That is not my subject, highly interesting though it is. My main reason for introducing the L-fields – absorbingly fascinating in their own right – is to make a first move into the immaterial and to show that there is already a complete involution at the immaterial physical level. As Burr says, 'The cytoplasm of the living cell is not a formless conglomeration of chemical substances, but is an integrated and co-ordinated system. It is impossible to conceive a cytoplasm as a haphazard arrangement of molecules. A definite pattern of relationships must exist.' This relationship continues on between cells and is acted on and acts upon the force field of the whole body. This in its turn is embedded in all the other fields round about and these have to fit into the total field of the universe.

Burr conducted a series of long term experiments to see if it was possible to pick up the influence of any extraterrestrial forces on living things here on earth. It seemed fairly clear from work so far that one major input into the formation of the voltage gradient was the charged particle distribution in the living system, the chemical flux of the system. In order to establish whether there were any external factors, Burr carried out experiments over a period of 30 years with electrodes set in the growing layer of tree trunks. The experiment was extended to include the air and earth near one of the trees. It very soon became apparent that, although the magnitudes were different, the trees, the air and the earth all showed variations in the potential difference at the same times. In this particular experiment the trees used were an elm and a maple, together with the earth and air nearby. Records taken over a long period of time made it clear that a change in one of the subjects was accompanied by a change in all the others. It will not perhaps seem too surprising now, in view of what has already been said about the fields of individual systems being embedded in wider fields which are ultimately embedded in the total field of the universe, but it was found in this experiment that there were changes in all four subjects related to such things as diurnal cycles, lunar cycles and things like sunspot activity and magnetic storms. More sunspot activity meant an increase in voltage gradient and vice versa.

In an earlier chapter I made the point that computers do not act on their own any more than a spade digs the garden on its own, and that a dead brain is nothing more than a collection of chemicals, even though materially it is just the same organ as when it was working in someone's head. In similar vein I would submit that DNA *per se* is no more than a collection of chemicals and does not directly cause us to be what we are. In a way analogous to the computer and the brain it is the spade that digs the garden and not the gardener. It is the channel through which the life force can act in a particular way. Chemistry provides the motive power and is the source of the necessary energy. However, chemistry requires direction and according to Burr it is the electrodynamic field which determines the direction in which the energy provided by the chemistry in a system will flow.

The above has been a brief and broad-brush look at what was perhaps a rather unexpected initial approach to the question of involution. It is an entry point that is not too daunting because, although we are dealing with the intangible, we have been dealing with electrostatic fields and this is a familiar branch of physics. However, this is by no means the whole story. In my early digression on a way of viewing the Trinity I characterised what seemed to me to be the three major facets of our universe. These are energy, the manifestation and fixation of energy and consciousness. Now we come to the time to widen the net to include consciousness and indeed we have already come to its borders with mention of psychosomatic illnesses and the like. Many of us are quite happy with the mechanical part of physics but feel uneasy with electricity because you cannot actually see where the wiggly amps go. The psyche, I fear, is like that only more so.

THE INTANGIBLE NO-OSPHERE

Nowadays one frequently hears the comment that the world is getting smaller. Of course this doe not mean that the globe is physically shrinking but that it seems relatively to be a smaller place than it was; and this is fair comment. We only need to take ourselves 250 years back in time to become vividly aware of this. If you wanted to go somewhere you walked or rode a horse. There were some variations on this theme such as the sedan chair, where you sat while other people walked, or the carriage, where you sat on a seat behind the horse instead of sitting on it; but effectively the means of transportation were walking and riding. This drew horizons in very sharply. The basic node point in the network of labour across the countryside was the village. People lived in villages who worked on the farmland round about. These people walked to work. The village also housed the artisans needed to support the labours of those who lived in the village and walked to work. Examples that spring to mind are the smith, who tended the feet of the main source of power and also did whatever metalwork was required, and the carpenter, who would probably also have to turn his hand to coffins and wheels and cider barrels as well as chairs, tables, carts and the frames of houses. Because everything had to be within walking range of the village, this meant having a village every 3 miles or so. Trade between villages, the sale of cattle and sheep and horses and surplus produce took place in the market towns. These were set at a distance apart such that the people in their catchment area could, as a rule, make the journey to market and back in a day. This dictated that they must be something like 10 to 15 miles apart. It would be a rare occurrence for the average person to go beyond the nearest market town in each direction and this meant that the land beyond the far side of their catchment area was unfamiliar territory about which information was sketchy and irregular. The immediate horizon was at a radius of about 3 miles from the village centre, the far horizon at a radius of about 30 miles and beyond that lay foreign parts, heard about in tales of tinkers and drovers and coachmen. The larger administrative districts of countries of that era were generally based on the area which it had been possible for the local feudal baron to control effectively, given the existing communications. The larger regions still of nations and empires had an inherent tendency towards disintegration and fragmented into *de facto* autonomous regions unless there was a strong leader in the centre. Uprisings and civil wars were commonplace. The decaying Holy Roman Empire spawned over 300 principalities and states in the region of Germany. It took an outstanding leader to overcome the handicap of inadequate communications.

Then, one after another inventions occurred which began to impinge on the *status quo*. In this country in the 1840s came the railways and the Royal Mail. The camera was also developing. I still remember the surprise I felt on first seeing photographs of the battlefields of the American Civil War, but workable cameras were already upon the scene. Ships now had steam engines and the development of the internal combustion engine brought ever increasing numbers of motorised vehicles on to the roads of the country from about the beginning of the 20th century. There was also the telephone. If you lived in Southampton in 1750 and wanted to visit your aunt in Newcastle it was a major undertaking involving many days of travel. It was certainly not something that you would expect to do frequently. Regular communication of any sort would indeed have been quite difficult. 150 years later you could make the journey in a day; you could correspond as a matter of routine through a quick and reliable mail service; and it was even possible to speak to Aunty on the telephone. If in 1750 you had wanted to go not to Newcastle but to India the journey would have taken several months by sailing ship, with periods of extreme discomfort, not to say danger and uncertainty. 150 years later a steamship would have taken you there in a matter of weeks. The expansion of horizons caused by these innovations was patchy and by no means universal, but the effect was ever increasing. Very soon after this came radio and pasenger-carrying aircraft. Improvements in travel and communication followed one after another - television, satellite communication, computers and even personal and laptop computers, fax, modems etc. The effect of each of these innovations is very small at first, but gradually it gathers momentum. The telephone, the motor car, the aeroplane and so on only affected a very small proportion of the population in their early days. What a difference there is now! It is now normal to have a telephone and a car. What is more, the motor car of today is not the underpowered, unreliable machine of the get-out-and-get-under days of yore. It is a machine in which our Southampton resident could quite easily, barring snarl-ups on the M25, drive up in a day on the motorway system to visit Aunty in Newcastle. Thanks to the internal combustion engine, the village has completely lost its original reason for existence. We no longer actually need villages. Mechanised agriculture has reduced the numbers working on the land to a tiny fraction of what they used to be. The proliferation of cars and vans and pickups and buses means that it is now rare for anyone to walk to work. Artisans providing support for the economic life of the village catchment area are also a vanished race. One does find many of their successors still living in villages – although they might just as well live anywhere – but they are now self-employed builders and electricians and plumbers and welders who travel over a wide area. Where you live is now much more open to choice. Many people living in villages nowadays live there for the fresh air and sense of space and travel daily to work in towns. Still other people live in villages from choice and work in 'electronic cottages'. It is possible to carry on many occupations anywhere at all where one can plug in a computer, a fax and a modem. There is enormous physical involution in the world of work.

Aeroplanes were also for the few in their early days. Their use is now so widespread and, with the multiplying effect of charter flights and package tours made possible by a system of organisation aided by computers, something like 6,000,000 people from UK fly each year to Spain alone. Once upon a time we bored our friends by showing them our holiday snaps: now we can show them life as it happened thanks to our camcorders. Even better than that, we can be anywhere in the world in real time thanks to TV and satellite links. If the government wished to send instructions to the Governor of India 100 years ago it was a long winded affair. If it wishes to communicate with the Ambassador in Washington now, he can be reached immediately by telephone and written instructions can be sent instantaneously by fax and electronic mail. The video telephone is on the way.

It is small wonder that we say the world is getting smaller. Travel is easy and commonplace. Communication in various forms with anywhere at all is instantaneous. It is a far cry from the 3 mile radius horizon of the villager of 250 years ago. Ease of more widespread communications in both the sense of travel and the sense of information exchange make large scale administration increasingly possible. On the commercial level we have international banking, which reaches even to the ordinary person by international credit cards, and international companies that are completely interlinked by their computer networks. Large political units become possible and we can see moves towards this. First of all there was the tentative League of Nations and now there is the well established United Nations – although the time is perhaps still too early for true cohesion on such a scale. Closer to home we can see the result of increased communicative capability pushing us on inexorably towards a federal Europe. Another thing that becomes apparent as one surveys the advances in travel and communication is that the pace is always accelerating and, indeed, the the rate of acceleration is always accelerating. Where shall we be in 100 years time? Where indeed!

So here we have a very visible involution of the world, a turning in on itself. What, if anything, is the invisible correlate of this? Underlying the visible and the detectable but invisible manifestations of energy (eg radiomagnetic waves) is consciousness. It is what de Chardin calls 'the Within'. Perhaps another thing we could call it is the power of the think-act. We have seen that evolution is the story of a rising complexification which is accompanied by a rise in the level

97

of consciousness. It has become apparent that consciousness can only show itself to the extent that the vehicle for this exists. De Chardin makes the point of what he calls the 'loss of the peduncles'. He says that by the time we become aware of a change it has really reached a relatively advanced stage, but that when we try to follow it back to its origin the tracks are already obliterated. Using this same line of thought he says that by the time we are aware of consciousness at an obvious level in living organisms its development has already been going on for a considerable span. He says that there is a Within to things that is co-extensive with their Without and that 'refracted rearwards along the course of evolution, consciousness displays itself qualitatively as a spectrum of shifting shades whose lower terms are lost in the night'. He feels that matter is in principle conscious matter but that its consciousness can only manifest itself as it becomes more and more organised. He goes so far as to say that with the individualisation of our planet a certain mass of elementary consciousness was originally imprisoned in the matter of the earth. That is a bold assertion to which we may have to return, but I think I can see why he makes it. If consciousness is the power of the think-act and its effect is revealed in energy and the manifestation of energy then it may be fair to argue back the other way and say that this particular quantum of energy and its fixation and manifestation is associated with a particular quantum of consciousness. I hear what he says, but it need not necessarily be so completely limited. We have seen in looking at L-fields that the whole structure of the universe is integrated and interacting. However, in the matter of the rise of consciousness he says in other words – and many more of them – essentially the same as I have been saying, namely, that consciousness shows itself as the matrix of matter permits.

CONSCIOUSNESS, COMPUTERS AND T-FIELDS

I intend to abandon any investigation of the peduncles of the research into consciousness and start boldly in with the work of Sigmund Freud (1856–1939). He qualified as a doctor and began his professional career as a neurologist. From this he went on to study the functional aspects of mental disorder. It had been found by Breuer that neurotic symptons might be successfully removed by putting the patient under hypnosis and making him recall the painful emotional experiences that had been repressed and had given rise to the symptons. Once the cause of the symptons was recognised and discussed it was possible to alleviate the effects. Freud applied this treatment successfully to hysteria; and this starting point for his work coloured and indeed stunted its progress. The disorders that he dealt with were caused by repression of some experience from the consciousness of the patient. Freud extrapolated from here to the idea that anything that went from our being actually conscious of it was repressed from our consciousness because we did not want it to be there. He also came to the conclusion that these repressed and unfaced experiences were normally something to do with a sexual impulse, usually in the context of family life.

Moving on from his clinical work with neurotic people to a general theory, Freud divided the mind into repressing and repressed parts. Put another way, there was a conscious and an unconscious part. In moving on to these general concepts he really was in uncharted waters with very little to help him. One is reminded of Leibnitz reaching the stage where he needed to be able to talk about energy at a time when nobody had defined such an idea. He tried to make three levels or subdivisions of awareness. Firstly, there was the conscious. Then there was a pre-conscious where an idea was latent and he described it by saying that the idea was unconscious only descriptively and not in a dynamic sense - whatever that means. Thirdly, there was the unconscious, which was the dynamically unconscious repressed

99

– whatever that means. Put another way, in the mind there was a conscious and an unconscious part. The repressed part was unconscious, but he also postulated an active unconscious that influenced conscious thought. His vision of it, as he felt his way into this unknown field like a blind man tapping with his white stick, is a great deal less than crystal clear, but he was astute enough to infer from his clinical work that there is a coherent organisation of the mental processes from what he calls the Ego, to which consciousness is attached. When he considered the Ego further he decided that part of it must be unconscious but not latent like the pre-conscious because it could never become conscious. Under the personal Ego, ones organising and co-ordinating self, he put the Id. This was the seat of the Libido, the force of the primitive unconscious. He ended up by incorporating all of this in a drawing that looked something like a squashed haggis, with the conscious at the top, the pre-conscious underneath it, the Ego underneath this, the Id at the bottom and the repressed part pushed round the corner.

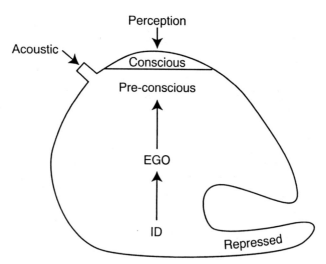

A Freudian View of the Psyche

He really was in uncharted waters and so was trying to build up a theory from clinical cases. In a way he was situating the appreciation. He said he had found very powerful mental processes or ideas that could produce all the effects in mental life that ordinary ideas do although they never became conscious. There was no framework on which he could hang ideas of this nature. Presumably it was his working from empirical cases that gave rise to his quaint, even ridiculous, fixation on sexuality. The Id was sensual and sexual and constantly seeking self-gratification; it had to be controlled by the Ego, responding to the need to come up to the standard set by the Super-Ego or Ego Ideal. Freud postulated that all people have an active unconscious which influenced their conscious thoughts and behaviour. Drawing on his clinical work, he argued that the unconscious elements are split off from consciousness because of conflicts within the psyche arising from feelings and ideas that the conscious mind found unacceptable and therefore repressed. He wrote, 'Why ideas cannot become conscious is that a certain force opposes them, so that otherwise they could become conscious.' He argued that this repression was linked to infantile sexuality, particularly the attraction to the parent of the opposite sex, the so-called Oedipus Complex. Freud carried out much work on the Oedipus Complex and its resolution. He stated his general conclusions as follows, 'The broad general outcome of the sexual phase dominance by the Oedipus Complex may therefore be taken to be the forming of a precipitate in the Ego, consisting of these two identifications [mother identification and father identification] in some way united with each other. This modification of the Ego retains its special position; it confronts the other contents of the Ego as an Ego Ideal or Super Ego'. He is somewhat at a loss as to how to handle the presentation of these ideas and finds it easier to personify the Super-Ego, Ego and Id and have them negotiating or even conversing with each other. He said that the Ego dreaded the Super-Ego, the voice of conscience. He wrote, 'The Superior Being, which turned into the Ego ideal, once threatened castration, and this dread of castration is probably the nucleus around which the subsequent fear of conscience has gathered; it is this dread that persists as the fear of conscience'. They must have been an odd lot in Austria at that time! For Freud it is sexuality that drives everything and the Id is the repository of the Libido, which is a general and undiscriminating sexual drive that feeds into the Ego.

Freud's conception of personality was blinkered by his complete concentration on the sexual impulse as the force of the unconscious and this has latterly been recognised. It is of course very true that childhood sexual experiences can be a cause of problems in later life, but there is more to us than that. He also had something of a fixation on the intra-psychic dynamic of human personality and did not give due weight to the effects of inter-personal and social relationships on human development. That said, his enormous contribution to thinking was not simply in the field of psychoanalysis, where he was one of the true pioneers, but also in his attempt to obtain some vision of the levels of the psyche, thus paving the way for Jung

The vision of the psyche was clarified and extended by Carl Gustav Jung (1875-1961), a Swiss doctor who specialised as a psychologist and psychiatrist. Jung joined forces with Freud and others in the International Psychoanalytical Society, but by 1913 he had outgrown Freud's sexual straightjacket and moved off on his own. Indeed it could be said that he ended up with a diametrically opposed slant to Freud in that he came to feel that one must aim at the integration and harmony of the whole psyche and that this was something which was particularly a challenge for the second half of our lives.

However, I am not really trying to set out Jung's views as a psychiatrist but rather to describe the way in which he promoted and advanced thinking on the no-osphere. If we look at the psyche from what we might call the apex down, at the top you have the *persona* of the individual. This was originally the mask worn by an actor to show who he was. It is the front which a person presents to the world. As Jung put it, '*Persona* is the individual's system of adaptation to or the manner he assumed in dealing with the world. Only, the danger is that people become identical with their *persona* - the professor with his textbook, the tenor with his voice. One could say, with a little exaggeration, that the *persona* is that which in reality one is not, but which oneself as well as others think one is.' Below this come the other parts of the self, the conscious, the sub-conscious and the personal unconscious. Writing on consciousness Jung said, 'When one reflects upon what consciousness really is, one is profoundly impressed by the extreme wonder of the fact that an event which takes place outside in the cosmos simultaneously produces an internal image, that it takes place, so to speak, inside as well, which is to say: becomes conscious'. One calls to mind Freud's haggis drawing, with the acoustic and other perceptions feeding in from the exterior into the conscious and the pre-conscious feeding in from the inside. Writing of the unconscious, Jung said, 'Everything of which I know but of which I am not at the moment thinking; everything of which I was once conscious but have now forgotten; everything perceived by my senses, but not noted by my conscious mind; everything which, involuntarily and without paying attention to it, I feel, think, remember, want and do; all the future things that are taking shape in me and will at some time come to consciousness: all this is the content of the unconscious...Besides this we must include all more or less intentional repressions of painful thoughts and feelings. I call the sum of all these contents the personal unconscious.'

Below the personal unconscious Jung postulated something much more exciting than Freud's Id, whose frantic sexual appetites were for him the force driving the primitive unconscious. Jung postulated a collective unconscious. He said that over and above the personal unconscious 'we also find in the unconscious qualities that are not individually acquired but are inherited, eg instincts as impulses to carry out out actions from necessity, without conscious motivation. In this deeper stratum we also find the Arche-types. Instincts and Arche-types together form the collective unconscious. I call it 'collective' because, unlike the personal unconscious, it is not made up of individual and more or less unique contents but of those which are universal and of regular occurrence.' He noted the recurrence of motifs which crop up again and again and again in the myths and fairytales of world literature. He met the same motifs in the phantasies and dreams and delusions of living individuals. He said, 'They impress, influence and fascinate us. They have their origin in the Arche-type, which in itself is an irrepresentable, unconscious, pre-existent form that seems to be part of the inherited structure of the psyche and can therefore manifest itself spontaneously anywhere at any time.' I think it is fair to say that Jung had perceived and made a first description of the no-osphere.

It is much easier to talk and write about this sort of thing nowadays than it was when Jung was writing about it. There are two reasons for this. The first is that there has been time for us to become acclimatised to this amazing vision. We think nothing of saying that we will feed a difficult problem into the mincing machine of our subconscious for the night and hope that the answer will be ready by the morning. We find this as simple a viewpoint to express as in earlier times we would have said, "I'll sleep on it". The terms 'conscious', 'sub-conscious' and 'unconscious' are ones we have grown used to. The other great reason why it is much easier for us is the advent of the computer.

The computer gives us a marvellous analogy that was not open to Freud or even Jung when they were setting out their vision of the psychological ambience. It makes the whole concept much more readily intelligible to us. For example, I am typing this on a PC. When I am working on a document on this PC only one page worth of it at a time appears on the screen. We can think of this as being analagous to the conscious part of the topic we are thinking about at a given time. We might liken the rest of the file in use as subconscious. We can look on the rest of the files on the hard disc as being analogous to my personal unconscious. There is even something that mirrors the repressed part of the unconscious which Freud pushed into the tail end part of his squashed haggis; this is the Recycle Bin. When I drop a file in the Recycle Bin, the document name is removed from the list of files in the folder in which it was located but it is not actually erased from the disc altogether. Instead of this it, the document is sent into the limbo of the Recycling Bin and it stays in limbo unless specially recalled. This seems a very close parallel indeed to the way in which we try to erase a memory by repressing it and pushing it as far away into our unconscious as we can. A file in the Recycling Bin cannot be drawn upon in the simple way in which other files listed on the disc can be drawn upon. A special extra procedure has to be carried out to make it possible to bring the file from its limbo on to the screen and in a similar way hypnosis had to be used to bring repressed ideas and feelings forward to the part of the psyche from which they could be brought up into the conscious. Another major parallel between my psyche and my PC is that in my unconscious there are instincts, while every time I use the PC I give it the equivalent of instincts by activating the Disc Operating System, its *modus operandi*, which is contained in that software. The analogy runs on beyond my psyche and my PC. Through the modem in my PC I can link into data networks. Files from other sources can be received directly into my PC via the modem and it has access to a vast pool of information. It is easy to see the analogy between this and the collective unconscious which affects the personal psyche. When Freud and then Jung were postulating levels of the psyche reaching down from conscious to unconscious and repressed and to external forces affecting the psyche in parallel to the external sensory perceptions it was a concept that had no peg to hang on in the experience of the people of that time. Now any of the millions of people who deal with computers in their daily lives are in constant contact with a structure that is a powerful and vivid analogy of what the pioneers described.

The other analogy which we have to make is between the materially manifest and non-manifest. Among the materially manifest I do of course include anything that can be detected and measured in physics, even if its energy is not fixed in matter, such as electricity and light. I have already discussed the electromagnetic L-field, researched by Professor Burr. L-fields are analogous to the DOS of a computer.

However, they are not the consciousness of the programmer. They are physical phenomena and are limited to the physical. In similar vein, thinking of examples of wisdom, truth and beauty causes electrical activity in the brain, but this activity is not itself wisdom, truth and beauty. These abstract concepts exist in reflective consciousness, in the no-osphere. They are non-material and cannot be detected by our physical instruments. People like Canon Andrew Glazewski routinely talked of T-fields, T for thought, as well as L-fields. He regarded the T-field and the L-field together as the organising field. In a lecture to the radionic association he painted an intriguing picture of their operation. He said that if we looked at part of our body, such as the hand, and magnified it so that the nucleus of an atom was the size of an apple then the next atom would be over 1,000 miles away. If we looked at our bodies on this scale it would be like looking at a universe, with billions of galaxies consisting of trillions of atoms. Even one biological cell would contain many galaxies of atoms. Yet something makes these billions of galaxies cohere together and work in an organised way towards a given goal. The moving of a finger is a striking illustration of the power of thought over matter. Glazewski says that it is the T-field which does the moving, using the energy of the atoms, which power the L-field. Although it may be helpful to regard the T-field, or however we like to describe thought, as an immaterial structure analogous to computer systems, we cannot measure it in material terms. However, it seems reasonable to me to accept the existence of the no-osphere and I find the computer analogy helpful in visualising it.

Reasonable though it may be to accept the real existence of an immaterial no-osphere, this is another major step in this essay. Yet if we go back to basics what do we find? We find Subsistent Being, who is personalised energy – or power, if you like, or even activity. He contains 'virtually' within himself the means of expressing this power in any way at all, even in ways that we could not possibly imagine. In our universe the power of the think-act that created it becomes apparent to us in forms of physical energy and matter, a reversible fixation of energy, which we can detect with physical apparatus. This is what science does and this is all that science can do. Recalling some of my previous allusions, it can detect the spade but not the gardener, the computer but not the programmer. As I have just said, thoughts of wisdom, truth and beauty are accompanied by detectable intra-cellular activity and detectable electromagnetic waves: but intra-cellular activity and electromagnetic waves are no more than that; they are not thoughts of wisdom, truth and beauty. Physically detectable material things are contingent and temporal. They are no more than forms of manifestation of essential power, which is not limited to such manifestations. They only started to exist with the Big Bang at "Let there be light" some 15 billion years ago: From all eternity before that Subsistent Being is. Thus permanent reality is to us intangible, undetectable, immaterial.

Centuries ago the physical sciences were included as one branch of philosophy, and that seems to me to be the correct perspective. They are about a particular field of knowledge, the field that can be observed and detected and measured and analysed, but it would be unreasonable to expect natural science to provide an overall, comprehensive system of knowledge. There is no question of a conflict between science and philosophy or between science and religion. It would be a matching not of like with like but of part with whole. Science does of course loom large in our daily lives. It provides us with aircraft to take us to the sunshine; it gives us pills to take away our headaches; it gives us instant food and microwave ovens; it gives us the pleasures of books, films and television – and so on and so on. It deals with a huge and ever increasing volume of knowledge. However, philosophy is by definition the love of knowledge and the natural sciences are just one branch of knowledge. Similarly, religion is about our relationship with Subsistent Being, while all that is physically detectable in this world is no more than the manifestation of part of the power of one think-act of Subsistent Being. If primary existence and fundamental reality are not limited to the material, are indeed immaterial, and if the no-osphere is as real as the geosphere –

107

and indeed controls the physical – then recognition of this fact is of fundamental importance for further meaningful advances in knowledge and understanding.

REINCARNATION, THE SOUL AND THE BODY

A topic that people have always found fascinating is that of the possibility of reincarnation. The Buddhists are quite certain that it happens and the Christians are quite certain that it does not. There are many ancient writings on the subject. The Egyptian book of the dead dates back to about BC 1300. Its title, 'Going Forth in Light', is reminiscent of modern near death experiences (NDEs), of which more later.

Another well known book on the subject of reincarnation is the 'Tibetan Book of the Dead' (*Bardo Thodol*), an 8th century book about the plane of consciousness between earthly incarnations, which the Tibetans called the *Bardo*. According to this book, the life between lives lasts for a nominal 49 days and the experience there ranges from the bliss of being completely enveloped in radiant light to a meeting with a judge, the Lord of Death, who sifts through the record of good and evil acts reflected in his Mirror of Karma. The Ancient Egyptians believed that they lived in pleasure in *Amenthe* between incarnations. The Australian Aborigines believed that the soul took up its abode in some object of nature such as a tree, a rock or a pool of water in between incarnations. There is even a reference to reincarnation in Plato's 'Republic', when a man called Er comes back to life 12 days after being killed in battle and gives an account of the life between lives; he tells how each soul could select the form of its next incarnation; and he says that before taking up the next incarnation each soul had to drink from the River of Forgetfulness to erase all conscious memory of past lives. This enforced forgetfulness not unnaturally crops up elsewhere, too. I say 'not unnaturally' because we do not have any normal awareness of a previous existence and this lack of consciousness of any previous life has to be accounted for. Further common features of the between-life state include a sense of timelessness, envelopment in a wonderful light and an assessment of the soul's performance in the incarnation that has just ended.

Regression under hypnosis is now one of the techniques of psychoanalysis and there are many cases available as a result of many years of research. One such case history was that of a Canadian woman called Paula Considine, which was researched by Dr Joel Whitton. He carried out weekly hypnotic regression sessions with Paula for an extended period and she described for him a long succession of incarnations, including one as a girl born on a farm in Maryland in 1822, another as a housekeeper near Quebec born in 1690, another as a nun born in 1207 who worked in a Portuguese orphanage, another as the younger sister of a tribal leader in Mongolia under Genghis Khan and another as a slave girl in Ancient Egypt.

Now after what I have already said about the no-osphere it is evidently not necessary for the person who is now Paula Considine to have actually existed previously as all these remembered characters in order to be able to describe their lives. The analogy of the computer is again helpful here. On the storage discs of computer networks there is a mass of files put there by all sorts of different people. They can be drawn upon by anybody who has access to the network. In an analogous way, we spend our live creating files for the no-osphere. The Existentialists say, 'Je suis mes actes', but I find it more reasonable to think that I am my consciousness. Now if all the files that we create with our consciousness are eventually stored on the hard discs of the collective unconscious there is no reason why, given suitable circumstances, they should not be accessed. The use of hypnosis to enable us to access files stored deep in our personal unconscious is commonplace. The cornerstone of Freud's treatment was the recall of the infantile experiences which had caused the problems in later life. It therefore seems not unreasonable to me that some people at least can access under hypnosis beyond their personal unconscious down into the files of the collective unconscious.

A more intriguing aspect of this is the concept of the *Bardo*. Dr Whitton carried out much detailed research into this which took him into territory not covered by NDEs. Perhaps I should mention NDEs first before going further into the *Bardo*. There has recently been a lot of interest in NDEs and various articles have been published and TV programmes made. The usual pattern is that the persons who are on the point of death find themselves looking down on their apparently dead bodies. Then they enter a long tunnel, at the end of which there is a light that gets brighter and brighter and closer and closer. Sometimes the subject finds himself back in his body without reaching the end of the tunnel: at other times the subject passes out of the tunnel into a wonderful place of light and love, with a sense of peace and disembodied floating. There is considerable general similarity between the narratives, with differences in the detail. It is normally a happy experience, leaving the subjects convinced of the continuance of consciousness after death and taking away their fear of death. The people who have these NDEs are not of any particular social or educational or religious background or of any particular age. For example, the subjects in an article in the Daily Telegraph magazine were the Head of the United Nations World Literacy Programme, who had his NDE when he was badly wounded during the war, a lady who nearly died during a brain operation, another lady who is a office administrator, who nearly died in childbirth, and a 64 year old retired steelworker who suffered a heart attack. They made comments such as, "When my Mum was dying, I wanted to tell her, 'Mum, you'll really enjoy it'" or "I'd love to have that experience again" or "But the day will come when He (Christ) won't turn me back. I won't be frightened to die now. I'll go up there. I know I will. He's been good to me once and He'll be good to me again".

As the term Near Death Experience implies, all these people returned to the body that they had come so near to leaving permanently. Their experiences tally with what is described in the ancient writings already mentioned. What of those who do not come back? What about the *Bardo* and its correlates in other religious traditions? Dr Whitton stumbled into this field by accident during his hypnotic regression researches. One day Paula Considine failed to regress back to the next previous incarnation that she was expected to describe. She said that she was up in the sky looking down on her mother, who was heavily pregnant with her. When asked her name, she replied that she had no name. It appeared that Dr Whitton had by chance hacked into the period between two previously described incarnations some 55 years apart. He has since explored regressed memories of discarnate existence with more than 30 subjects. They were struck with awe and amazement and struggled to describe the wonders of their discarnate surroundings. Dr Whitton described the state into which the subject entered after passing through the tunnel and coming out into the light as 'metaconsciousness' a state of memory awareness in which the recipient loses all sense of personal identity by merging into existence itself, only to become more self-aware than ever. As the subjects entered the metaconscious state, every sign of fear, anxiety or pain that had accompanied the death experience disappeared. Their faces became peaceful and then filled with wonder. As one subject described it, "It's so bright, so beautiful, so serene. It's like going into the sun and being absorbed without any sensation of heat. You go back to the wholeness of everything. I didn't want to come back." Another subject said, "Everything makes sense; everything is perfectly just. It's wonderful to know that love is really in control. Coming back to normal consciousness, you have to leave behind that all-encompassing love, that knowledge, that reassurance. All is love."

The normal experience of the subjects was that they were met by a guide who led them in front of a tribunal where their life was reviewed. After that the next task in the discarnate state was to plan the next incarnation. Helped by the advice of the tribunal members, the next incarnation was planned, for example, so as to overcome defects that had not yet been overcome or to enlarge the total experience of the soul. Finally, as I have already mentioned, all memory of the *Bardo* and of past lives is wiped away before reincarnation.

It is a fascinating story. Dr Whitton's subjects had certainly hacked into something and it was something whose initial stages corresponded to what has been reported in the NDEs of people who have come back to life from the point of death. I do not, however, find it reasonable to accept that the hypnotic suggestion and instructions of a living man should be strong enough to over-ride the erasing of memory carried out by supernatural beings before reincarnation. Perhaps the subjects were able to go so far down through the collective unconscious that they reached the absolute bedrock of the essence of the power of the think-act. I do not know. It is a fascinating and awesome field of research.

This leads me to a few musings – and they are no more than that – about the soul. First of all I ought to attempt some sort of definition of what I mean by the soul. The simplest one that I have ever heard is that the soul is what makes us what we are. This applies to all animate beings, plants, insects, fish, animals, man, and the soul is the immaterial organiser and source of continuity. It is the part of Desscartes that knew that he was thinking. It organises the body through the matrix of the L-field by the mechanism and energy of the physical cells.

Now if we consider the soul to be that which makes us what we are, it is very plain that is changes during our lifetime. You only have to think of Shakespeare's seven ages of man. A new-born baby is very like a puppy or any other new-born mammal. It has instincts and consciousness, but there is no sign of reflective consciousness. Tests were recently carried out on some of the anthropoid apes using a mirror to see if there were any signs of reflective consciousness. The researchers came to the conclusion that, of the animals tested, only the chimpanzee was aware that it was looking at its own reflection. Rather to their surprise, the gorilla was not. This led them to the conclusion that chimpanzees have a certain degree of reflective consciousness, which is an interesting thought in itself. Now I do not suppose that if you put a mirror in front of a new-born baby it would know that it was looking at an image of itself. Once again we have the problem of the loss of the peduncles; and by the time we realise that in infant has developed a degree of reflective consciousness the process is quite advanced. Certainly I believe that most people would agree that by the time an infant says its first word it has developed a degree of reflective consciousness. This then develops through life until old age is reached. Then the faculties gradually begin to fail until ultimately the person is, as Shakespeare concludes, 'sans everything'. We have seen during the discussion of the rise of consciousness that the Within can only express itself through the organisation of matter with which it is presented. The level of consciousness rose as cerebralisation increased. Thus in the lifetime of man we can see the rise and fall in the level of reflective consciousness.

This leads on to a reflection on the immortality of the soul. The first line of the argument for the immortality of the soul is straight from Plato's 'Republic'. When I look at the first proof of the immortality of the soul in my school notes from so many years ago I see that it says, 'Since the soul is spiritual, it is able to exist even when separated from the body; and since it is simple it has nothing within itself which is a source of corruption or death. Therefore the human soul is naturally immortal.' This is the 'lack of specific evil' put forward by Plato. He noted that disease or injury or lack of food could damage or even kill our bodies. He found that material things were undone by some specific evil, but he was unable to find a specific evil which could affect something spiritual like the soul. He therefore concluded that the soul was immortal. Yet it seems at first sight that the soul can only flourish and express itself insofar as it can do so through the body. The Penny Red says that the three powers of the soul are the memory, the understanding and the will, and these can be seen to be linked to bodily capability. Is the decline of the body through which it acts therefore the specific evil of the soul? If the soul is immortal, is it immortal in the 'sans everything' state or in the state it was when the body was in its prime? Is the body simply used as far as its faculties permit as one of the many vehicles for expression of an integral Within?

I would like to suggest a possible answer based on what has already been said about the no-osphere. First of all, however, I would like to say that I find it reasonable to accept that the soul is personal and not an impersonal manifestation of the total Within. The one thing that Descartes's malicious demon could not take away from him was his knowledge that *he* knew when *he* was thinking. He knew from this that he existed as a person and this is our common experience. It seems perfectly reasonable to me. This person, as Jung pointed out, is made up of everything from the top of his personal consciousness to the lowest levels of his personal unconscious. Using the computer analogy, a person is everything from the document of which a part is on the screen, corresponding to consciousness, to all the files in his personal disc storage - all the ideas and thoughts and memories - and all the software of instincts and the like. In the case of the computer, that remains whatever the state of the hardware. It also remains even if all the files are copied on to the hard disc storage of a central network database, analogous to our thoughts and ideas and experiences being incorporated into the collective unconscious.

It would thus appear that the soul has an immaterial existence in the no-osphere and acts in the material sphere through the body. This would mean that it is indeed unaffected by deterioration of the body and that it would retain all the experience and development achieved throughout the life of the body. It would also mean that the soul is essentially a free agent, able to exist beyond space-time if necessary.

Other questions and speculations spring to mind. For example, does the completion of the material pattern at conception trigger the programming of its correlate in the no-osphere – the human equivalent to the 'booting up' of a PC, with all the instincts, reflexes and common knowledge of the human unconscious? This would enable appropriate control and direction of the material development of the person and would also provide the enabling mechanism for personal development throughout life. It is not so far-fetched an idea as it may seem at first sight. Consider the example of the nesting habits of birds. These are many and very varied, but a bird of a given species will inevitably make the nest peculiar to its species quite irrespective of whether or not there are other similar birds to give it a model.

I feel that this whole line of thought about the soul might fruitfully be developed further.

Another interesting and associated subject for reflection is that of the resurrection of the body. This is one of the things in which Christians state their belief every time they say the Creed. There has always been a dichotomy in our thinking about what happens at death. On the one hand we acknowledge that the soul continues to exist and that the person concerned continues to have uninterrupted conscious existence. There is an illustration of this, for example, in the parable of Lazarus and Dives. On the other hand we persist in making reference to a primitive old idea that the dead sleep in their coffins until wakened by the Last Trump at the end of time.

'Each in his narrow cell forever laid,
The rude forefathers of the village sleep'

and so on. There are splendid medieval paintings full of ghastly figures wreathed in shrouds climbing out of their coffins as an angel sounds the last trump and awakens the dead, who have presumably been slumbering in their coffins in some state of suspended animation. All very graphic. However, the mechanics of such a literal interpretation are more than a little complex. It is said that all the people in the world at present would fit on to the Isle of Wight, but they would not actually be able to do anything beyond standing there like vertically canned sardines. What on earth would it be like if all the people in, say, London who had ever died there all came back to life again and tried to live there? It would be absolute chaos. Also, each generation lived in a different London as it changed over the years. Would Saxon villagers have to camp out in part of the Lloyds building? It is an absurd way of putting it, but I am simply trying to indicate that there is more to it than everybody simply opening up their coffins and coming back to life. Would there have to be a number of different worlds set at different points in time? If so, people would be cut off in a slice of their lives. Their parents or their children

116

might be in a different world. Would time go forward, or would the moment stay for ever? Would we be involved in another space-time that simply went on and on and on? Some of the problems with that have been touched on already. How old would we be? How old would our parents be? Our children? Then there is the 'Ilkley Moor Baht 'At' factor. Much of the matter that made up our bodies will have been re-used and re-used and re-used. What seems a very simple statement turns out to be extremely complicated. There is a far more serious consideratiaon than the rather facetious ones just mentioned for wondering about the resurrection of the body. Would there be any need for bodies as we now have them? Our bodies are the material means with which we contribute to the rise of consciousness and involution by acting in space-time. Time is one of three inextricably interlinked parameters – speed, time and distance. If time has ended and there is no more time, then this is also the end of space-time. If we are talking, as we presumably are, of a situation where space-time has ended, what need would there be of bodies? It is customary to talk of the last trump being sounded 'at the end of time'. If space-time ceases to exist, the stage for our bodily activity ceases to exist. Thus physical bodies and the end of time are mutually contradictory. The subjects of Whitton's research described themselves as being in a floating state, but they were still conscious of themselves as persons. So were the people who had NDEs, who did not seem to have any particular need of a body in the situation in which they found themselves. It seems possible that on being confronted with the full reality of Subsistent Being we might lose interest in all the transient things of this world, even chocolate biscuits and good malt whisky, and simply be transfixed for ever with a shout of amazement and exaltation on our metaphorical lips. One might say that bodies are for doing, not being. What would we need to be doing for all eternity? Physical actions are tied to time because they have a beginning, a middle and an end. The 'Penny Red' says, 'By 'the resurrection of the body' I mean that we shall all rise again with the same body at the day of judgement'. Why? What is the relevance of a body if there is no space-time? I must confess that I do not understand in detail what the significance of this is. Does anyone? It certainly seems to be a concept that could well bear some clarification and amplification.

THE ULTIMATE CULMINATION

In the preceding chapters we have eased ourselves into the immaterial or spiritual. We did this first of all by looking at L-fields and T-fields. Then we availed ourselves of the work of psychoanalysts, notably Jung, to take a view of the human psyche and of consciousness as an entirety. This is the no-osphere, the sphere of the νουσ, the mind. We can appreciate its existence from seeing its effects. It is not a whit the less real because it is not capable of measurement by material scientific instruments. I said at the outset that when confronted with a possible choice I would always take the option that seemed to me to be the more reasonable. Well, it seems thoroughly unreasonable to me to accept that fundamental reality is totally contained in what is detectable in this universe, which only came into existence some 15 billion years ago as a result of external power. Fundamental reality, Subsistent Being, is not detectable *per se* by us; we know of it through its effects.

As has been mentioned before, man is more than the sum of the protons, neutrons and electrons of which he is physically made. They are the power house and the agents, the gardener's spade, not the gardener. It is really loose talk, for example, to say that a particular gene causes a particular effect. It does, but only in the sense that when a chef uses a pastry cutter of a particular shape he will duly cut out pieces of pastry of that shape. Held in the directing matrix of the L-fields, the chromosomes are the code by which inherited characteristics are handed on from generation to generation, the channel through which the no-osphere acts. In this sense it is indeed true to say that genes control our characteristics; it would, however, be wrong to ascribe to a collection of chemicals the capability of being wholly responsible for personality. The flow is the other way. Schopenhauer deduced that the stuff of the universe was energy but, because we tend to associate energy with its manifestations such as heat, it would perhaps be safer to describe the stuff of the universe as power, the power of the Within, the power of the think-act. This power or vir-

119

tual energy is manifest in the various forms of physical energy and in the fixed form of matter. That is the flow, or so it seems to me.

As an illustration, let us consider briefly the question of male and female. There are 46 chromosomes in the human cell and only a particular one of these has to be different to change the gender. The sexual characteristics are carried on special pairs of sex chromosomes, the human male having one X and one Y sex chromosome (heterozygous) and the female having two X chromosomes (homozygous). These X and Y chromosomes are the tools by which the body is directed to grow into a female shape, with child bearing and child rearing organs and secondary female characteristics such pelvic shape, a voice that does not break at puberty and little facial hair, or a male shape, with seed producing and delivering organs and the normal secondary male sexual characteristics. However, that is by no means all there is to being male or female. There has been a movement in recent years which has sought to convince us that we are all just people, that we are all born the same and that boys and girls are brainwashed by society into adopting the respective male and female personalities. What utter rubbish! I have read time and time again the rueful lament of mothers who discovered from personal experience how fallacious was this beguiling theory. These educated, liberal women took great pains that there should be no bias at all in the early experience of their children. And yet the time came when the boys put their dolls aside to shoot at each other delightedly with toy guns or to hack at each other with toy swords. There used to be a simple expression that summed it all up, 'Boys will be boys'. There is indeed a brainwashing, but it is a brainwashing by instinct built into the no-osphere over millions of years. There is much in the human male instinct that is common to other male animals. There is an underlying behavioural commonality among such disparate animals as the bull and the lion and the baboon and the robin. Quintessentially it is the instinct to control territory and females and to hunt or gather where this is appropriate in order to continue the species. There is little basic difference between the battles of rutting deer over does in a wood and the battles between young human males over human females outside a disco on a Friday night.

Brainwashing there is, but by far the strongest part of it comes from the instincts embedded in the files of the collective unconscious in the no-osphere. It is indeed possible to persuade people to oppose these instincts and perhaps if this process were to continue over sufficient ages then we might be able to stamp out psychic maleness and femaleness; but to deny the innate difference currently programmed into us by the no-osphere is absolute tosh. There is a simple and well known description of these primeval urges that grew along with evolution and are a relic of it; it is 'the Old Adam'. Could it just possibly be that the notion of Original Sin has something of a common origin with this?

If we look again at the rise of complexification, first of all there was the aggregation of particles into the simplest atoms of hydrogen and helium; as the temperature eased and matter stabilised and aggregated further, the more complex atoms were formed. These atoms then became the building blocks for molecules. The minerals were left behind at this stage, but molecules based around the chemistry of carbon became the building blocks for polymerisation into megamolecules. These in their turn became the stepping stones to living cells. Once again the cells became the component parts for the building of more complex living organisms until a stage of complexification and cerebralisation was reached where thought burst upon the world and consciousness was achieved. With the advent of consciousness we have the first humble beginnings of the building of the no-osphere, but this began to leap forward in an unprecedented way with the attainment of reflective consciousness in man. The no-osphere entered into a different order of complexification with the advent of reflective consciousness. The radial force of evolution had brought our world thus far at a constantly accelerating pace. If we have now entered the era where consciousness is folding in on itself under the tangential force of involution, whither is this leading us?

121

What is going to happen as the building of the no-osphere progresses? What is going to happen in the end?

This is where modern philosophy disappoints. In ancient times a philosopher was both an abstract thinker and a physical scientist. While observing and measuring the world round about, he tried to fit his discoveries into a universal whole, a macro view. With the post-Renaissance, post-Reformation Age of Enlightenment, scientists became split off from the stream of abstract thinking and concentrated on analysis. It seems that they really believed that a sufficiently detailed analysis of the world round about us would reveal its inmost secrets. And indeed there were countless startling discoveries which added bit by bit to our knowledge of how the world round about us works, how and when it was formed, what its operating rules are. All sorts of things were revealed. Combustion was combination with oxygen, not phlogiston going out of a substance. Blood went round and round our bodies in a special circulatory system. Great discoveries were made and laws established by men whose names have now been enshrined in the names of units associated with their discoveries, men like Joule for work, Pascal for pressure, Ohm for electrical resistance, Hertz for frequency, Faraday for capacitance and Newton for force. Scientific knowledge became more and more detailed, as did the analysis of the world around us. At last there came the electron microscope, which allowed us to see things in such detail that it must surely be possible to capture all the secrets of science and philosphy? These appliances have indeed given us immense amounts of useful knowledge that can be and is being applied in all sorts of ways. However, ever more detailed analysis is scientifically fascinating but has proved to be a philosophically sterile path. It leads back downwards to molecules, atoms, electrons and ultimately to energy as the basic physical stuff of the universe, a fact realised by Schopenhauer some 200 years ago. The world around us is plainly more than the sum of its tiny parts. Unfortunately, modern philosophers seem to have lost heart. Philosophy seems to have been prone to wither and degenerate in proportion to the advance of science, until we reach the stage where Wittgenstein held the chair of philosophy at Cambridge and propounded obscure theories that were treated with reverence in spite of – or was it because of? – their incomprehensibility when all the time he was mad. 'Nuff sed. Science has made more and more amazing leaps forward, but philosophers have become progressively less able to use the discoveries for synthesis into a coherent and convincing overview of how the whole thing gels. It beggars belief that more and more detailed understanding of what has been created should be taken for a reason for dispensing with the need for a creator. If I take my motor car engine to pieces until I understand completely how every little piece of it works, does it make me think that, just because I understand it, somebody else did not have to build it? Do I say that it must have made itself? When I was a student I remember jocular reference being made to a certain divine who was said to have remarked, "This morning I heard a bird sing, so I know there is a God". His remark was elliptical, not stupid. During his training he had absorbed the arguments from motion, causality, order and so on so thoroughly that he skipped without stating them from the initial observation of the bird to the final conclusion of the existence of God. Elliptical, but not stupid. It would unfortunately seem that people in modern times lack the necessary basis on which to build and incorporate the analytical discoveries of science into a coherent synthesis.

Fortunately there has been one man this century, and to my knowledge only one man, who has been in a position to unite science and philosophy and who has attempted a synthesis. Teilhard de Chardin was a scientist of formidable intellect who taught physics and geology and who was a world-famous paleontologist, as outlined earlier: but he was also a Catholic priest - a Jesuit at that – and so was thoroughly versed in philosophy and theology. What is more, he constantly related one to the other. He was a latter-day Rennaissance Man, a Compleat Man. In attempting the synthesis of scientific discoveries into a philosophical coherence, his position and qualifications must be well-nigh unique. There is, however, a particular problem with de Chardin (quite apart from his literary style). In an effort to avoid antagonising the ecclesiastical authorities too much and perhaps in the hope that they would one day relent and allow him to publish his writings (in fact they did not; and he, in obedience, kept his work unpublished throughout his life): he wrote 'The Phenomenon of Man' as a scientist and 'Le Milieu Divin' as a Catholic priest. It is therefore necessary to read the two in conjunction (and indeed also to include his comments in 'Letters from a Traveller') in order to see the full richness of his vision.

Where did de Chardin think that the future was going to take us? He looked forward to 'mega-synthesis' and 'hyper-personality'. Mega-synthesis is a neat way of expressing the fact of bringing things together, collating, incorporating and integrating them into a single unit.

When it comes to looking at the arrival of thought or reflective consciousnes upon the scene, there is the usual problem of the loss of the peduncles. There seem to have been a number of developments enjoying a varied amount of success on the borders of intelligence. The great apes certainly stand right on the borders of thought. I mentioned earlier that chimpanzees can recognise their reflection in a mirror as being that of themselves. I note that a book ('The Pinnacle of Life – Consciousness and Self-awareness in Humans and Animals' by Professor Derek Denton) reviewed in a more recent newspaper article (DT 13/10/93) makes the same claim for gorillas and other un-named (in the review) great apes. Palaeontologists have discovered tantalisingly rare evidence of other species which are morphologically between the great apes and *homo sapiens*. At the end of the Lower Pleistocene period we find chipped stones on almost all the raised lands of Africa, Western Europe and Southern Asia. Well over one million years ago there are the remains of the primitive Australopithecus. Then moving on in time we come to Pithecanthropus of Java and Sinanthropus of China. Anthropologists agree that both of these types are definitely hominid in their anatomy. Their skulls fit in between those of the great apes and *homo sapiens* and they had an erect biped posture. Peking Man of about 350,000 years ago is known to have used fire, enabling him to live in caves in the relatively cold area of North China. Moving further on in time we come to Neanderthal Man, who spread widely throughout NE Africa, the Near and Middle East and Eastern Europe from about 110,000 years ago to about 30,000 years ago, when he was eclipsed and supplanted by Cro-Magnon Man, our ancestor. Neanderthal Man typically dwelt in a cave and wore clothing of skins. He used sophisticated tools and weapons and he buried his dead. With Cro-Magnon Man of the Upper Paleolithic Age of from about 30,000 years ago we find such things as cave paintings, ornaments, a variety of clothing and much greater sophistication of dwellings, tools and implements. It is thought that they almost certainly had a spoken language. However, there were still relatively few of them. Ice Ages came and went and man had to move with the climate. Numbers were increasing and prey was being hunted to extinction, but is was only with the end of the Ice Age about 10,000 years ago that man was able to settle down to farming, growing crops and domesticating animals. With this change and with the consequent rapid increase in numbers we have the start of civilisation proper. Prior to this the peoples would only have been groups of loosely bound wandering hunters. It is only when we come to the Neolithic Age that we come to permanent settlement of land and the filling up of territories on a permanent basis. As the areas favourable to settlement became filled and spreading out became complete, then physical and psychic involution began its course of acceleration. I suppose that if the earth had been flat then the human race would have spread out and when groups reached the edge they would have been forced over by the pressure of those behind. That is rather a fatuous idea, but I just want to point up how useful it is that the earth is spherical, a closed shape. As there was nowhere to go, the mounting pressure had to turn inwards. The fundamental change from hunting and gathering to agriculture brought all the other changes in its train. There is an Oriental saying, 'Neighbours are for ever'. If you have to live with the same group of people in the same place it is necessary to develop a scheme of communal rights and duties, laws about property, kinship, moral taboos and marriage and laws of socially acceptable conduct. Stability gave scope for things that were well nigh impossible for people constantly on the move. It was in Neolithic times that we see the development of pottery and weaving, the beginnings of metallurgy, the first attempts at written language, and of course the development of all aspects of agriculture. The collective memory, the collective unconscious began to develop apace. The no-osphere began to develop apace and to envelop the closed shape of the earth.

We have already anticipated this by looking in an earlier chapter at the frantically accelerating pace of involution in the period immediately preceding the times in which we are living now. Now we have come to a world of large political units and even global organisations like the United Nations and the Red Cross/Red Crescent. In the psychic correlate of this physical organisation the collective unconscious becomes more and more unified, drawn together as a result of the plethora of modern communications from the telephone to the facsimile to the radio to the television to the internet. The closed geometrical roundness of the earth, which closed everything in on itself from the earliest times, was a necessary feature generating the first syntheses and polymerisations. It has sustained the radial force of evolution in the Biosphere. Now it is forcing coalescence in the correlate no-osphere. With man we have moved to another plane. Ramifications before the advent of man, the fanning out of a phylum, were at a physical level: ramifications with man, if there are to be any, are at a psychic level.

So we have seen that the story of evolution is that of the rise of consciousness. Now we can see that the rise of consciousness is to result in effecting union. We have seen progressive physical union as evolution developed. There was the union of thousands of atoms in the polymers of the carbon compounds; then there was the cell, which contained thousands of molecules, all linked together; then came more and more complex living organisms that integrated millions of cells.

Now, with the advent of thought, the Within takes over to reinforce integration of living organisms in an enormous psycho-biological operation which de Chardin called mega-synthesis. An interesting point is that mega-synthesis is apparently the result of tangential forces, but, as happens with all advancing stages of organisation, this gives the capability for moving forward in the radial direction, moving forward on the main axis of evolution towards higher levels of complexity and, in this case, higher levels of consciousness.

The direction of the thesis is now becoming evident. Involution produces the evolution of consciousness or knowledge. We can see this very simply if we stop to consider the vast data banks of knowledge and the vast physical size of the resources now available to research. And involution also, as we have seen, draws together. If we produce the line of the flow of involution on to its ultimate then the no-osphere ultimately converges at what de Chardin calls the Omega Point. This is mega-synthesis.

There is, however, another side that has to be fitted into this. We have to fit in the personal. As mentioned elsewhere, the only thing that Descartes's malicious demon could not strip him of was his knowledge of himself thinking as a person. This is our common experience by which we are aware of the fact that we are not identical with or part of a joint person formed with those round about us. We are aware of ourselves as individual persons. Analysis, that instrument by which so many strides have been made in science, is a progressively depersonalising thing. If we examine closely the structure and working of individual cells in the human body, we increase our knowledge of the parts but we have descended below the level of operation of the human person to which these parts contribute. If we analyse far enough we come down to energy, and I am aware of being more than an inanimate package of energy. The constant thrust of evolution has been the rise of consciousness through complexification. If we were to believe that the future lies in the diffusion of our personal consciousness into a universal totality of energy that would be a movement diametrically opposite to the historical flow of evolution. The culmination of the ascent to consciousness should, I submit, be supreme consciousness and supreme personal consciousness. The attainment of personal consciousness has been the highest achievement of evolution to date and as involution progresses so consciousness should rise to more perfect heights.

De Chardin goes on to consider the problem of the association of an Ego with the totality of the All. By possessing consciousness we become capable of centring everything constantly in relation to ourselves and in so doing we come into association with the other centres round about through our senses and our reason. In the psychic involution of which we have experience to date we can see the signs heralding the birth of a single centre made from the myriad of individual centres. This convergence point of the hyper-personal centres is of course the Omega Point. Whether or not de Chardin would approve I do not know, but for myself I have christened it the Orchestra Point. I find this helpful as a musician for forming my own perception of the Omega Point. Many years ago when Sub-Lieutenant of the Gunroom of HMS Ark Royal (the one with the angled deck, not the one with the ski-jump) I played the trombone in her volunteer military band. 26 of us used to assemble to practice in a 4-berth cabin. The trombones had to sit on a top bunk so that their slides had freedom to go in and out. It was unity in plurality. We each played our own parts but we were aware of what the others were playing and each made our contribution to a centred whole. It may have sounded like hell to the poor people next door, but to us there it was utter ecstatic harmony that must be the nearest thing to heaven on earth.

De Chardin is not easy to read. He coins neologisms liberally to describe ideas for which there are no adequate existing words. He uses metaphors which hope to give a transient impression but which are not capable of analysis. How, for example, could one make a concrete analysis of the statement that the soul is 'the incandescent surface of matter plunged in God'? He builds on what sometimes seems to be a succession of far-fetched metaphysical assertions. Yet he arrives at the Omega Point, where all the hyper-personal becomes centred in the All. Is not this hyper-personal amazingly coincident with what has been described in the context of NDEs as meta-consciousness, a state of memory awareness in which the recipient loses all sense of personal identity by merging into existence itself, only to become more self-aware than ever? As one of Dr Whitton's subjects said, "It's like going into the sun and being absorbed without any sensation of heat. You go back to wholeness of everything. I didn't want to come back". There we have the consciousness of oneself and the consciousness of the All. There, I think, we have a description of Omega, the convergence of all consciousness and all the conscious. ' The Phenomenon of Man' was written in the 1930s and, apart from a short section at the end, the author wrote as a scientist and natural philosopher. However, much of the thinking in Book Four, Super-Life, is based on a vision set down as a Christian theologian and philosopher a decade earlier in 'Le Milieu Divin'. Thus when he wrote about the Ultimate Earth in 'The Phenomenon of Man' he already had in his mind the religious vision of it from his earlier writing. When writing as a scientist, his views on what actually happens when the Omega Point is reached are guarded. As the centre of all consciousness and hyper-personality, Omega must be personal; and as the end of the series of our progression, as the Great Stability, it must at the same time be outside all series. It is the conscious Pole of the world, transcending the consciousness converging on it. It is the Great Stability, which is to be found not by diffusion downwards through matter to energy but upwards through consciousness to meta-consciousness and hyper-personalisation.

What happens in the end? For what it is worth and in all its resounding opaqueness, this is how de Chardin sees it. In 'The Phenomenon of Man' he writes,

'Now when sufficient elements have sufficiently agglomerated, this essentially convergent movement will attain such intensity and such quality that mankind, *taken as a whole,* will be obliged – as happened to the individual forces of instinct - to reflect upon itself at a single point; that is to say, in this case, to abandon its organo-planetary foothold so as to shift its centre on to the transcendent centre of its increasing concentration. This will be the end and the fulfilment of the spirit of the earth.

The end of the world: the wholesale internal introversion upon itself of the no-osphere, which has simultaneously reached the uttermost limit of its complexity and its centrality.

The end of the world: the overthrow of equilibrium, detaching the mind, fulfilled at last, from its material matrix, so that it will henceforth rest with all its weight on God-Omega.

The end of the world: critical point simultaneously of emergence and emersion, of maturation and escape.'

Writing as a Catholic priest in 'Le Milieu Divin', he is more visionary and less guarded.

'What is it, when all is said and done, the concrete link that binds all these universal entities together and confers on them a final power of gaining hold of us?

The essence of Christianity consists in asking oneself that question, and in answering: the Word incarnate, Our Lord Jesus Christ.'

By Christ he is thinking of the link between the eternal and almighty God and the limited universe of space-time forged when that God physically entered into space-time in the person of Christ and who thus became the contact point between God and this think-act of his. When no-ogenesis and involution have progressed to the ultimate,

'the tension gradually accumulating between humanity and God will touch the limits prescribed by the possibilities of the world. And then will come the end. Then the presence of Christ, which has been silently accruing in things, will suddenly be revealed – like a flash of lightning pole to pole. Breaking through all the barriers within which the veil of matter and water-tightness of souls have seemingly kept it confined, it will invade the face of the earth....Like lightning, like a conflagration, like a flood, the attraction exerted by the Son of Man will lay hold of all the whirling elements in the universe so as to reunite them or subject them to his body.'

So, if I have some glimmer of understanding of his meaning, the whole of completely involuted reflective consciousness goes out of space-time and the remaining dross, energy or energy fixed as matter reverts in a mighty nuclear cataclysm to being part of the infinite power of Subsistent Being. There is an old hymn that starts, 'I rise from dreams of time'. Cunning old Shakespeare has a line, 'We are such things as dreams are made of'. Perhaps the best analogy for the whole universe may be that it is a daydream of God. Perhaps.

SPECULATIONS ON HELL AND FREEWILL

In a rare sermon on Hell, a venerable and learned old priest said that there are 18 references to Hell in the New Testament, 12 of them being made by Christ himself. I take his word for it! Some of them are very well known, like the section in Matthew 25 about separating the sheep from the goats and the wicked departing into everlasting fire.

The concept of Hell is not without its difficulties. Imagine, if you will, that you own an extensive estate surrounded by a high, secure wall. In this estate you plant woods and dense thickets of bushes. You lay out paths all over the estate, some of them leading to dead ends in thickets or bogs or pitfall traps. You also position other pitfalls, snares and booby traps along all the paths. You introduce further dangers such as carniverous beasts and poisonous snakes into the estate. There is just one entrance and one exit on the far side from it to which the correct path eventually leads. You then go and kidnap some unsuspecting person, push him in through the entrance to the estate and bolt the door behind him. Before leaving him you give him a thorough briefing on what he will find inside the estate and how he can avoid the dangers. You also give him a rifle and other weapons necessary to protect himself from the live dangers inside. You tell him that if he reaches the exit successfully he will be given a million pounds. Then you settle down to watch his progress on closed circuit television. At first he does quite well, but in the process of avoiding a particular danger he takes a wrong turning and thereafter he becomes more and more confused. Eventually he is overcome by weariness, falls asleep and is eaten by a crocodile. "Poor chap," you say, "He didn't follow the brief." Do you think that the general opinion would be that your actions had been just? I submit that you would be held to be guilty of illegal killing because the man did not volunteer to go into your estate and face the dangers. If you had told him of the prize and of the dangers and he had made the free choice to attempt the passage through to the exit, that would have been a different matter: but in actual fact he was frogmarched to the gate after the briefing, hurled inside in spite of his protests and screams, and the gate was slammed shut behind him.

We do not ask to be born. We arrive screaming in this world whether we like it or not. Now it is always claimed that our good qualities are reflections of the good qualities inherent in God and that our sense of justice is a reflection of the infinite justice of the Almighty. If we think that what you did as the owner of the estate was unjust, as I think we all would, then it seems hard to reconcile this with accepting that anybody who does not come up to snuff in his progress through this life will be punished for it eternally. I do not have an answer for this; I merely point out the rather anomalous situation.

De Chardin does not seem to find the idea of Hell an easy one. In 'Le Milieu Divin' he writes, 'You have told me, O God, to believe in Hell. But you have forbidden me to hold with absolute certainty that any single man has been damned. I shall therefore make no attempt to consider the damned here, nor even to discover – by whatsoever means – whether there are any. I shall accept the existence of Hell on your word, *as a structural element of the universe*. The existence of Hell, then, does not destroy anything and does not spoil anything in the Divine Milieu whose progress all round me I have followed with delight. I can even feel, moreover, that it effects something great and new there. It adds an accent, a gravity, a contrast, a depth which would not exist without it. The peak can only be measured from the abyss which it crowns....Tearing open the nether darkness of the universe, you show me that there is another hemisphere at my feet – a very real domain, descending without end, of existences which are, at least, possible...I pray, O Master, that the flames of Hell may not touch me or any of those whom I love, and even that they may not touch anyone...but that for each and every one of us their sombre glow may add, together with all the abysses that they reveal, to the blazing plenitude of the Divine Milieu.'

The former Bishop of Durham, Dr David Jenkins, drew criticism for reportedly suggesting that Hell was all in the mind. Well certainly when we leave space-time we take leave of the physical. Flames and branding irons are not applicable. The only torments that are applicable are such things as unending remorse or impotent hatred. Nor is the idea a new one; it has, for example been deliciously explored by C.S.Lewis in 'The Great Divorce', with even a suggestion for the explanation of freewill in terms of relativity.

Hell would be even more unthinkable if we did not have freewill. To be predetermined from the outset for an unending future of pain and torment would be grossly unjust. However, the question of whether or not man has freewill is one that has caused continual argument. On the one hand there are those who say that if I come to a fork in the road I am completely at liberty to go either to the right or to the left and that this is a simple demonstration of the fact that I have freewill. On the other hand there are those who say that because of factors in my previous experience I may think that I am making a free choice but in reality the choice is made for me.

I have found it helpful to use the analogy of the fruit machine. Imagine, if you will, that you are standing in the bar of a comfortable pub with a pint of John Smith's or a gin and tonic or whatever is your favourite tipple ready to hand. You are standing in front of a fruit machine that has the usual 3 wheels with symbols of cherries and lemons and plums and so on and a lever on the right hand side to set it in motion. It also has 'hold' buttons for each of the drums, a 'nudge' button, buttons for selecting various prize options and a chart of additional prizes illuminated rapidly in turn by lights. If you have cherries on two of the drums you can hold them and try to get a cherry on the third drum only. You can work away furiously at the 'nudge' button when it becomes operative. You can use any of the controls available to you in any way you wish. You have absolute freewill, genuine freewill, in this respect. However, the fact remains that the overall result over a long period of time is predetermined by the way in which the mechanic sets up the machine. No publican would give a fruit machine house room if there was any chance that he was going to end up losing money. The fruit machine is set up to pay out a certain percentage overall of the money that is put into it.

This is a simple example of the co-existence of predetermination and freewill and this analogy can be carried over into our daily lives. A fairly straightforward example to examine is that of reproduction. Every individual is intellectually free in his approach to sex. Everybody is absolutely free to marry or not – or in these days to form a so-called stable relationship or not. With present day knowledge and facilities every pair of partners is absolutely free to choose when and if to have children. Some people choose not to marry. Nuns choose not to marry so that they can dedicate their lives entirely to the service of God. Some people do not like the idea of sex; some do not wish to lose their freedom; some are attracted only to their own sex; some are too shy to make a positive move. For whatever reason, some people do not form a *de facto* married relationship and every individual person is free to choose not to do so. The same applies to having children for those who are physically capable of having them. Yet although each individual has absolute freedom of choice, it would be a complete ethnic disaster if everybody decided not to marry and have children. The human race would simply come to an end. Yet we do not worry about this coming to pass because, as we all know, our sex drive is powerful, second only as an instinct to that of self-preservation. Like the programming of the fruit machine, this piece of our programming makes sure that, *overall,* people do wish to copulate in sufficient numbers. A maternal instinct – and possibly even a paternal instinct – allied with curiosity about what the resulting child might be like ensure that enough people see the job through and have children. There is even a degree of fine tuning. Solomon had a thousand wives – or 700 wives and 300 concubines, to be more precise – and the Twelve Tribes of Israel were fathered on the two sisters who were Jacob's wives and their two maids. There was a need to fill the empty spaces and build up the people. Onan came to grief when he refused to act for his dead brother and give his widow her quota of children. When Christ came he ordered monogamy and so slowed down the build-up, which had by then progressed well. There is a natural check in that advances in science and medicine have on the one hand signally cut down the infant mortality rate but on the other hand they have provided reliable ways of limiting the size of families. Shakespeare said that in spring a young man's fancy turns to love, but for most young men this happens in spring, summer, autumn and winter. What is more, we have learned from sources such as the Hite report that the same applies to young women. This sexual urge is so strong that although every individual has complete freedom of choice, the actuarial odds are that the majority will produce offspring, pushed by that instinct which has been placed in our software for this very purpose, aided and abetted to a certain extent by the peer pressure which results from its effect. Just as in the case of the fruit machine we have individual freewill and overall actuarial predetermination. To my mind they validly co-exist and within this framework I see no contradiction between the co-existence of freewill and predetermination. Only I would have put Shakespeare's thought the other way round when he said, 'There's a Divinity that shapes our ends, rough hew them as we will'. It seems to me that the progress of the rise of consciousness is predeterminedly rough hewn, but that within this flow there is freedom for individual shaping.

There is something else that makes it seem more reasonable to me to think that we have freewill rather than that we do not. Imagine if you will that you are Subsistent Being – all powerful, omniscient, eternal, living in a great present tense. You have this wonderful idea for something different. You say, "Let there be light" and invent time, where things happen sequentially. So far, so good. However, if all these sequential happenings in this newly invented time are predetermined then the interest is limited. A small boy derives pleasure and interest from watching a model train go round and round an oval track, but the interest is hobbled. How much more interesting it would be to have the sequential events in time not predetermined but able to develop into a miriad of possibilities subject to a set of ground rules. If you were Subsistent Being and invented time, would it not be much more satisfying to add freewill rather than predetermine everything? Perhaps I should broaden this scope of possibility and describe it as an element of chance until the capability for thought developed and freewill thereafter. It seems to me that two of the fundamental pillars of this think-act are, firstly, time and, secondly, variety of possibility, the latter developing into freewill in man.

AGGIORNAMENTO

I would now like to move boldly from the plight of philosophy in this modern age to the plight of the Christian churches. One point that I would like to make at the outset is that illustrative examples are given which are just that, no more and no less. If I say, for example, that some rules have been relaxed this does not imply that I am calling for hair shirts and public penance.

During the last 30 years there has been a very noticeable fall in the numbers attending Christian churches regularly on Sundays. According to my newspaper, the weekly average Anglican congregation has now shrunk to a point where it is smaller than the Catholic one. I am told that the decline in Non-Conformist church attendance has been even more severe. Nor has the Catholic church any grounds for complacency because the falling away in the generations that have grown up since Vatican II has been nothing short of catastrophic. A very large majority of those of the younger generation who were baptised as Catholics go to church rarely, if at all. This is by no means the result envisaged for Vatican II. It was meant to be a rejuvenation, a renaissance. Pope John XXIII wanted to open all the windows and let fresh air blow through the edifice of the church. It had become apparent that the old-established structure and attitude were badly in need of some sort of face lift if they were to continue to enjoy the wholehearted and willing support of the faithful, especially the younger ones, and Vatican II was meant to result in a church that was in tune with the modern age. The operative word was 'Aggiornamento'.

The thought has occurred to me on more than one occasion that perhaps de Chardin was intended to be a sort of John the Baptist, a herald, for Vatican II. Perhaps he was meant to give an indication of the path to be followed in bringing the church into tune with an age of galloping scientific achievements. If that is so, the timescale was altogether too short. We must remember that Vatican II began many years before even the rehabilitation of Galileo and official accep-

138

tance that the earth went round the sun. De Chardin had been forbidden to publish his work during his lifetime and the few short years between his death in 1956 and the opening of the Council in 1962 were far too short a period for this work to be digested and effectively used. All those taking part in the Council had been raised on a diet of medieval philosophy which had continued virtually unchanged for hundreds of years and the great majority would have been suspicious or, worse, dismissive of the work of men like Darwin, Einstein and de Chardin. The Council generated a huge volume of paper which was of course unread by the vast majority of churchgoers. The results of the Council for them were what happened in church and what they heard from the pulpit. What was perhaps really startling was what they did not hear from the pulpit, especially from the new generation of priests that began to emerge from the seminaries after the work of the Council had been absorbed into a revised syllabus. One of the things most noticeable to the man in the pew was the avoidance of hard doctrine and the easing of disciplinary rules. Abstinence from meat on Fridays was abolished. Instead of having to fast from everything, even water, from midnight before receiving communion it was now only necessary to fast for 1 hour and water could be drunk at any time. Holydays, when all the faithful had to attend Mass, were reduced in number and could sometimes even be transferred to a Sunday. Sermons that impinged on difficult doctrines became rare. I mentioned earlier the doctrine of the Atonement, but Adam and Eve and the Garden of Eden were scientifically imprecise and made for an uncomfortable basis for preaching and were avoided. When the very old, venerable and learned priest whom I mentioned earlier preached his sermon on Hell, he opened his remarks by saying that it was a long time since he had preached a sermon on Hell, and that in fact it was a long time since he had heard anyone preach a sermon on Hell. Thoughts of Hell used to loom large in the background at funerals in the old days, with their black vestments and air of doom and gloom; but vestments at a present-day funeral are usually the white ones of joy and the service a thanksgiving for the life of the deceased, who is confidently assumed to be in bliss.

Rather than a great new perspective the first noticeable effect of Vatican II as seen from the pew was a watering down and a pushing into the background of anything difficult. Pre-Vatican II the Catholic church had been noted for its authoritarian certainty. Now it seemed to have lost its self-assurance and sense of conviction to an unnerving degree. People were invited to consult their own consciences. Rightly or wrongly, many people undoubtedly felt that the church accepted the fact that the old package was no longer tenable but did not really know what to do about it, and they felt that they might just as well go on their own sweet way without bothering much about the church any more.

One notable exception to the general abandonment of the line was that of birth control. I could hardly write about *aggiornamento* without some mention of this subject – and indeed it happens to be a useful and a graphic one close to people's hearts for illustrating how expanding scientific knowledge and capability has caused increasing pressure to be applied to the established ecclesiastical party line. I have kept many sorts of animals – dogs, cats, horses, goats, pigs, calves, and rabbits among them. Rabbits are the exception in this group. If a female rabbit is cervically stimulated she will ovulate 9 hours later. Rabbits have such a precarious existence that the male has the inbuilt impulse to copulate at every opportunity. This is not so in the other cases. Dogs will travel miles to a bitch, but only when she is in season. All these animals have some sort of ovulatory cycle and the fertile time is usually indicated by scent, visual signs and the willingness - indeed usually the eagerness - to accept the male. Goats come into season every 3 weeks during the winter so that after 5 months gestation their kids will be born in summer. Every 3 weeks in winter my goats dashed out of the shed bleating excitedly, grinning inanely and wagging their tails like clockwork toys as they looked round hopefully for a billy. You test whether or not a sow is ready for the boar by pushing on her back and if she will stand when you push down on her she will stand for the boar. Human females have an ovulatory cycle also, and it seems not unlikely that the frequent occurrence of pregnancy in young unmarried girls the first time they allow a man to have his way with them is because they feel most receptive at the most fertile time. Unlike dogs and goats and so on, however, we humans have worked out that sex is pleasant at any time, not just at the most fertile one. We have also worked out for ourselves the biological facts of reproduction and this knowledge has been applied for some time now to establish when the pleasures of sex may be enjoyed without their entailing the arrival of another child 9 months later. Our scientific knowledge is applied to achieve contraception. This avoidance of the fertile period is called natural birth control, or the 'rhythm method'. It is in fact rather cheeky to call it 'natural' since it is utterly unnatural, the natural thing being to copulate only at the fertile time, as I have pointed out. Another contraceptive method which makes use of our knowledge of biology and chemistry is the one where progesterone is taken as a pill by the female and this suppresses ovulation. In other methods we put a barrier between the sperm and the egg or use a chemical to kill the sperm before it can reach the egg. Vasectomy and tying the fallopian tubes can be regarded as forms of this barrier technique. All of these methods have two things in common. Firstly, they are deliberate applications of our scientific knowledge and, secondly, the intention in every case is to prevent conception. The Catholic church only accepts the rhythm method and has declared the others to be unlawful, but to the average man or woman in the pew – or in many cases because of this not in the pew – this seems to be no more than sophistry. The whole idea in every case is to apply knowledge in order to prevent conception except when it is planned and indeed the proponents of the rhythm method are quick to emphasise that it is just as reliable as the condom!! (In fact, this is a dubious claim because Burr's research has shown that some women ovulate over the entire menstrual period and that ovulation may occur without menstruation and vice versa. Detailed research in association with a number of hospitals

141

produced some unexpected results and, as Burr says, 'It helps to explain why the 'rhythm method' of birth control is inadequate'.) It was maintained that the cap or the condom interfered with the sexual act. They do not actually interfere with the sexual act but with the act of procreation, as does the rhythm method in its own way. At least mechanical methods of contraception allow couples to make love at the height of the fertile period when female libido is greatest. The rhythm method is indeed the most unnatural method of contraception because it forces couples to lie in bed in agonies of frustration on the very nights when they most want to come together. (Human weakness in the face of heightened libido is the other reason for failure of the rhythm method). The advent of the pill was watched with great interest. Our scientific knowledge was applied here in advance in such a way that there was no need for any interference at all during the actual sexual act. It has been reported that the committee appointed to deliberate on the rights and wrongs of the pill intended to give it the green light but that they were over-ruled by the Pope himself. There has been a series of articles entitled 'Beyond Vatican II' in the Catholic weekly 'The Universe' by Dr Eamon Duffy, who is a Fellow of Magdalen College and lectures in Church History. In an article on the pontificate of Pope Paul VI he wrote,

'From the outset of his papacy he set himself to hold together apparently irreconcilable radical and conservative forces. As a result, at times, he pleased nobody.

The most notorious example was his 1968 encyclical on artificial birth control, *Humanae Vitae*. He had established a Pontifical Commission of bishops, doctors, theologians and married people to review the whole issue. The final report of this Commission advised him that contraception was not intrinsically evil, that the Church's teaching on the subject, currently in doubt, was not infallible and could be reformed. Even conservative bishops like Cardinal Heenan expected a change. In the event, Paul drew back from appearing to contradict his predecessors and *Humanae Vitae* reaffirmed the ban on artificial contraception.

This was the worst of both worlds: to ask publicly for expert advice on a matter which affected the life of every married Catholic, and then to act against it. Typically, Paul softened the wording of the encyclical which conservative theologians had drafted for him. He removed all references to 'mortal sin', refused to claim infallibility, and inserted a passage urging confessors to treat married penitents with love and understanding. But, ironically, the ensuing row, and even more the fact that millions of Catholic couples ignored the Pope's teaching, realised Paul's worst fears about the loss of credibility for the Church's authority.'

Once again the average man or woman in the pew found it exceedingly difficult to understand why they could use drugs to regulate every single function of their bodies except ovulation. In the event the decision did not carry conviction. Many young people have left the church and continue to leave the church because they cannot accept the logic of it. The vast majority of the younger generation have not remained practising Catholics and this issue of contraception is one major cause. One can only think that many of those who remain or who have returned have come to a private accommodation with their own consciences. How many families of eight or nine or more – common two generations ago – does one come across nowadays? Modern medicine, hygiene and diet would make such large families easier than ever to accomplish – but they would also make such habitual numbers an ethnic disaster. Infant mortality is not what it used to be. My own father, for example, was one of six children, but his three brothers all died before they were six years old. The awesome power of the geometric progression is often not fully comprehended. If there were to be no contraception (or abortion) at all and all possible medical efforts were made to ensure that children survived to adulthood then families of 8 children or more would be commonplace and the population could easily quadruple every 25 years. If that happened it would mean that in 100 years it would have increased 256 fold i.e. a UK population of over 12 billion (roughly the present global population) and 100 years after that it would be 3 trillion. (The population of China would have become about 65 trillion). There are now ample numbers of human beings on this earth to build the no-osphere and go on to Omega, and any couple who have three children have certainly done their share towards ensuring continuity. This idea appears to be generally accepted by parents and all but a tiny percentage of families are small. The ovulatory cycle and the rhythm method were known about in the days when big families were common. Anyone who thinks that the disappearance of large families is due to the suddenly effective application of the rhythm method must also believe in Santa Claus. The birthrate in Italy is currently the lowest in Europe. Thanks to the Billings Method? Pull the other leg! A final thought that occurs to me is that omniscient Subsistent Being might just conceivably have set up the parameters of the world so that progress in civilisation and medicine that made a population problem possible would also yield an understanding of the control of fertility that would counterbalance this.

Of course this topic is also a good one for illustrating another bedevilling factor. This is the North-South divide over the way of regarding a rule. To a North European like a German, a rule is the bottom line; it is something always to be observed. To a South European like an Italian, a rule is an ideal to be aimed at. I had come to realise this many years ago and was not surprised to read in the Daily Telegraph of Cardinal Martini of Milan speaking in similar terms about contraception during his visit to England. He is reported as saying that the ban on artificial contraception is an "ideal" and that it was "more open to understanding" than people realised. Going on from there I would like to quote a passage in similar vein from a booklet published in the USA entitled 'How to Survive Being Married to a Catholic'. It is published by the Redemptorist Order and bears the *Imprimatur* of Bishop Anthony Emery. An *Imprimatur* means that it considered to be free from doctrinal and moral error.

On page 43 it says:

> 'The Church also understands the pressures that people may have to contend with in their lives and therefore takes into account not only what people do but also the circumstances that surround what they do. In other words the Church recognises that it is possible for someone to do something which, objectively speaking, is wrong but – because of the circumstances – the person who performs the action may not be personally culpable.
>
> This principle can be applied to the case of contraception. While no Catholic may reject any part of the Church's teaching or say that it does not apply in his or her case, there may well be circumstances in which a Catholic couple may conscientiously decide for unselfish reasons that they cannot increase their family and that the only option open to them is to practise contraception. In their circumstances this decision could be defensible.'

I do rather seem to have dwelt on this subject, but it is such a good general illustration of the sort of stresses that Vatican II has failed to remove or has perhaps indeed helped to produce. It is certainly a major cause of the absence of large numbers of people from the pews. The basis of discussion for many issues does not seem to have moved forward at all. There was another fairly typical example of this recently in 'The Universe'. This paper had a question and answer page where people could write in with questions about anything at all. Any reader who felt inclined could then send in a reply to the editor for publication in a subsequent issue. The reply that caught my eye on this occasion was one to the question 'Do animals go to heaven?'. The answer, sent in by a priest, was as follows:

> 'The answer is no. All living things have souls – the soul being the animating and vital principle of life. On earth we have three degrees of life: plant life, animal life and human life. An

animal has a soul that is mortal, finite; it dies with the death of the animal. An animal, therefore, has no potential whatsoever for life after death. Only humans possess an immortal soul, made in the image of God. Only we have the potential or possiblilty, by God's grace, of entering into the everlasting happiness of heaven.'

It is a straightforwardly pat pre-Vatican II answer. There are two didactic assertions: firstly, that there are three separate and distinct degrees of life; secondly, that the animal soul is mortal. The conclusion that the animal therefore has no potential for life after death flows naturally from these two assertions. However, these assertions may not seem completely satisfactory to someone whose studies and reading have extended to the 19th and 20th centuries rather than being limited to the 14th century and before. It may have seemed quite clear to Aristotle and Aquinas that life on earth could be divided into plants, animals and humans, but anyone with even a nodding aquaintance with post-Darwinian evolutionary biology is unlikely to see things in such black and white terms. As is illustrated by Cuenot's tree of life, evolution from the first cells to man was gradual and progressive. As de Chardin pointed out with his lovely expression 'the loss of the peduncles', the transitional points are difficult to establish because we only become aware of a new step when it has become readily distinguishable. It seems likely that amphibians evolved from fish that developed a fin at each corner, facilitating movement over tidal flats and shallows. At what point did such a creature cease to be a fish and become an amphibian? In a similar way, when we think of reptiles we may think of a King Cobra rising out of a basket as the snake charmer plays on his pipe and when we think of birds we may think of a swallow wheeling and swooping to catch flies in the summer evening. The division seems very clear, yet birds evolved from reptiles and there must have been a long transitional period when it was debatable whether the term 'reptile' or the term 'bird' was appropriate for a particular species. Even today, do we call the sea anenome a plant or an animal? There is likewise a blurring between man and animal. To the Greek philosophers and medieval Christian philosophers there would not have appeared to be any problem. By then the whole human race was *homo sapiens* and it was plain as a pikestaff what a man was. They did not know that it had not always been so. They did not know, for example, that prior to about 30,000BC Europe had been inhabited by *homo neanderthalis*. This was the product of a different branch of evolution from the one that produced *homo sapiens* and has died out; but Neanderthal man not only used weapons and clothes but also had art and language. Did he also have an immortal soul? He was the archetypal Stone Age Man with an established culture and would certainly be generally regarded as being human, yet a son of Adam he was not. If only the descendants of Adam, or, put another way, if only *homo sapiens* has an immortal soul, should there not be a recognisable difference between *homo sapiens* of 50,000BC and *homo neanderthalis* of 50,000BC? If *homo neanderthalis* had an immortal soul, what about Peking Man, *homo erectus*? He lived in communities and used fire. If Peking Man had an immortal soul, what about *australopithecus*? He used stone tools, killed with stones and stabbing sticks and made shelters. If *australopithecus* had an immortal soul, what about *ramapithecus* and the ape-men? Do we have to draw a dividing line somewhere in the middle of, for example, the development of *homo erectus* and say that all before this one were animals with mortal, finite souls and all subsequent men had immortal souls? Upon what do we base such an assessment? An apparent qualitative distinction between man and animals which springs to mind is that of the possession or not of reflective consciousness. Yet even this is not clear cut. As has been mentioned earlier, it appears that chimpanzees certainly and gorillas possibly have a degree of reflective consciousness. By possessing this attribute have they crossed the boundary from having a mortal soul to having an immortal soul? The rise of consciousness, the increase of cerebralisation, the progress of the tree of life has been gradual and progressive. One is reminded of what de Chardin said, 'Refracted rearwards along the course of evolution, consciousness displays itself qualitatively as a spectrum of shifting shades whose lower terms are lost in the night'. An educated modern person would undoubtedly find the first assertion in the letter an over-simplification. The second assertion, too, is a bald statement which does not even nod in the direction of Jung and those who came after him and engaged in research into the psyche. I need hardly say that it does not nod in the direction of de Chardin and the no-osphere. Yet an animal like a dog is programmed by a very complex 'Disc Operating System'. Also, a dog is undoubtedly capable of creating memory files. Like me, many people will have had the experience of meeting up after a long separation with a dog who was an old friend. The dog goes wild with delight. It remembers you. If human 'DOS' and memory files are a part of the no-osphere as an immaterial correlate of the physical human being, does not the same apply to those of a dog? If a human's immaterial correlate in the no-osphere is capable of existing outside space-time, does not the same apply to the immaterial correlate of a dog? I must confess that I rather incline to the opinion that when I come out into the light at the end of the tunnel my favourite black and white dogs will be waiting there to greet me. Be that as it may, the point I am trying to make is that this letter in 'The Universe' is a good example of why Vatican II was necessary and also of a dearth of change in the subsequent fundamental approach. The letter is based on pre-Enlightenment philosophical thought, which was the basis of pre-Vatican II Christian philosophy. Such an answer is not going to win the hearts and minds of educated people in this day and age and be accepted unquestioningly. It will be a source of exasperation. They will think it medieval, with a measure of justification. It will not help towards the regeneration of the Christian church. That such a letter with its philosophical basis unchanged from that of 50 years ago should appear in 'The Universe' 30 years after Vatican II shows that there is still much, very much to be done to achieve the *aggiornamento* that was the aim of Good Pope John.

If de Chardin was to be the herald of Vatican II and if this Council was intended to line up involutionary progress and direct it towards the Omega Point, then it is only natural that the intrinsic value of our life and efforts here should be highlighted. If we all regard this world merely as the ante-chamber to eternity, a vale of tears where we are put on trial, and if we all consider it a virtue to prevent ourselves from being tainted by the world by being absorbed in worldly things then involution is going to lack impetus. If we all take our footballs home, albeit from the purest and most blameless of motives, then the game cannot proceed. Strangely enough, the idea of the importance of the People of God did emerge from Vatican II, but it was divorced from the framework thought out by de Chardin. There was no clear explanation of <u>why</u> we and the world around us had become so important. The result when viewed from the pew was a big rise in the level of our self-importance and of our importance relative to God. Our sense of our relative importance went so far that the Anglican Bishop of London, Bishop Leonard, felt constrained to comment that we were trying to domesticate God. This may perhaps be illustrated by what has happened to the interior of Catholic churches and to the form of the Mass. Pre-Vatican II one was told that the church was the house of God, whose Real Presence was housed under the form of bread in the tabernacle. The priest as the appointed representative of the congregation stood in front of them facing the altar and tabernacle. His vestments and all the fixtures and fittings were the most costly and beautiful that could be afforded. Only the best was good enough for God.

The Mass itself, as was succinctly explained in the Penny Red catechism, was the repetition of the redeeming sacrifice of Calvary; a sacrifice was the offerring of a victim by a priest to God alone; the victim and priest here were Christ himself, with the human priest acting for him. A sacrifice required that the victim should be set aside and dedicated and consumed. It therefore followed that the essential core of the Mass was from the start of the Offertory until after consumption of the victim by communion by the priest. To satisfy the requirement for attendance at Mass on Sundays and Holydays one had to be in attendance throughout that period. It was reprehensible to miss the opening prayers and the readings and the sermon and the post-communion prayers and the prayers for Russia without good reason, but the essential duty had nevertheless been carried out. This was very clearly understood by the large numbers whose essential business prevented them from arriving until near the end of the sermon and forced them to leave as soon as the priest set down the chalice.

After Vatican II changes began to happen without any meaningful attempt at explanation. The first one of note was that the priest went round to the other side of the altar and faced the congregation, with his back to the tabernacle. The usual explanation, if any, was that it would be helpful for the congregation to be able to see what was going on, rather than have a back view of the priest muttering into his beard. It was also noticeable that a very simple wooden or stone table and plain, cheap vestments were the new vogue. It was almost as if the richness of the old vestments and the original altar and its surrounds were an embarrassing reminder of the crushing superiority of the Almighty. Then the tabernacle began to disappear from its central and focal position. It was put on a side wall or, if the church was big enough, in a side chapel. This feature was incorporated in the design of new churches. Over all the years of these changes I never heard a coherent explanation of what was happening from the pulpit. The reason may well be that the older clergy were anything from unconvinced to sickened by the changes and the younger ones felt that the less that was said the sooner their older parishioners would get used to the changes and accept them. It was not until about 25 years after Vatican II that I attended a liturgical seminar, feeling duty bound as organist to go along in case some of it affected me, and I then found out something of the thinking behind the changes.

One thing that struck me at the liturgical seminar was that the word 'Mass' seemed to have gone out of vogue. What happened now was that we came together to form the Assembly of the People of

God (the Assembly for short) to perform the Liturgy. The Liturgy was divided into the twin peaks of the Liturgy of the Word and the Liturgy of the Eucharist. These were now the two principal Liturgies and every effort was being made to make the Assembly feel that it was taking an important part in the Liturgy. As only a priest can perform the Liturgy of the Eucharist it meant that the relative importance of the Liturgy of the Word, in which anybody could take part, had to be stressed and inflated. The idea of the Mass as the repetition of the sacrifice of Calvary did not feature at all. The Offertory, which had been the first essential part of the sacrifice, was now the Preparation of the Altar and Procession of the Gifts and it provided an 'interlude' between the Liturgy of the Word and the Liturgy of the Eucharist. It was described as a bit of a low spot between the twin peaks where I might suitably fill in with some wallpaper music. I have to admit that it was a bit of a shock to the system. I could not help but feel that if people really believed that Subsistent Being became physically present in the transubstantiated bread and wine then that had to be the only peak worth mentioning. The words of Bishop Leonard about domesticating God came forcefully to mind. The tabernacle in which the Real Presence of Subsistent Being was housed was moved out of the way because it constituted a distraction from the complete act being carried out by the Assembly. I could not help but think wryly that Christ was already present himself when he carried out the first consecration. I hasten to say that there was no contradiction of basic doctrines; the transubstantiation of the bread and wine was acknowledged. It was the difference in approach, the difference in the vision of what we were about and the difference in relative emphasis which came as such a surprise. The priest was no longer drawn as the solitary, consecrated figure acting *in loco Christi*; he was now to be known as 'the Presider' and sit in the large chair where the tabernacle had been to preside over the Assembly. Moving the tabernacle also made it possible for the Assembly to gather together cheerful and chattering and conscious only of each other, not in silence and veneration, conscious only of the presence of the Almighty.

151

If you think about it, this is not a normal and natural way of carrying on. The temple of Solomon may be looked upon as fairly typical of the approach to designing a place of worship. Between the court where the general public gathered and the Holy of Holies that housed the Ark of the Covenant there was a veil, and only the priest was allowed to go beyond this into the Holy if Holies. Primitive tribes often worshipped the sun and here there was a similar approach to worship. The Incas built pyramid shaped plinths on which to place their altars high up towards the sun. Their geometrical shape prevented the whole throng of the people from standing at the altar. The Japanese worshipped the sun goddess Amaterasu Ohmikami, a mouthful that simply means 'Great honourable god who makes the heavens shine'. The sun was vitally important for making crops grow and ripen; and this wonderful power frequently made primitive peoples worship the sun. The Japanese thought it so important that they claimed that their Emperors were descended from this ball of incandescent helium and hydrogen. This religion has such old and strong roots that it imparts its flavour to the whole country and culture. The things that look like goalposts on the approach to Shinto shrines are called *tori-i*, which simply means 'bird is'. They are bird perches. Whether the legend arose as a result of a particular eclipse or whether, more likely, it grew up from the dark, overcast winter skies of Izumo on the coast of the Sea of Japan where successive waves of incomers landed after the crossing from Korea (the Pacific coast of Japan has a bright, sunny winter) I do not know. However, the joy of seeing the sun again gave rise to the story that Amaterasu hid herself in a cave; so some of the gods put on an entertainment outside to entice her out; when she came to the entrance of the cave, the sunlight shone out again and the birds nearby began to sing – hence the commemorative bird perches at Shinto shrines – and a strong god leapt forward and pulled her out of the cave – hence the origin of the enormous sacred white ropes that hang across the front of Shinto shrines and are also worn by *sumo* Grand Champions, the successors to the strong god who pulled Amaterasu out. In the grounds of the Imperial Palace, as

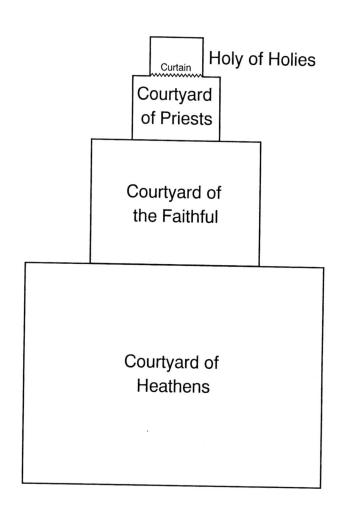

The Temple of Solomon

anyone who watched the wedding of Crown Prince Hiro will know, there is a shrine to Amaterasu with an outer hall, an inner hall and an inner inner shrine, the *nai-nai-den*, which only the Emperor may enter. Enshrined in it is the mirror in which Amaterasu is supposed to have seen herself as she came to the entrance of the cave. Once again there is no suggestion of having a large hall for everyone to meet in and chat while the sacred mirror is put out of the way in a side aisle. The concept is identical with that of the Temple in Jerusalem. And this is all for a mythical goddess who is not really taken seriously except as a vague symbol of national identity of an unspecified sort. How much stranger it is for the Catholic church with its seriously avowed belief in the Real Presence of Subsistent Being in the church to alter the layout in the way that it has. The gain is in human self-importance; the loss is in awe and reverence. The result is *hubris*.

It is hardly surprising that the result of this relative downgrading of the importance of God, together with the apparent loss of nerve and conviction of the church establishment (plus the stand on contraception that did not win hearts and minds) and the lack of any clear restatement that had obviously digested and reconciled the advances of science has lead the post-Vatican II generations to think that the church is not really worth bothering about much, a medieval relic, and that it has also lead to a sharp, potentially catastrophic fall in the numbers of those putting themselves forward to accept the hardships of life in the office of priest. This may sound like a harsh judgement, but the figures speak for themselves. It is not my judgement.

De Chardin was at pains to point out that our lives here on this earth have an intrinsic value and purpose in positively promoting the growth of the no-osphere and progress in involution towards the Omega Point, when all would be one in Christ. It seems to me that emphasis on our importance without such a reason being given for it is a highly significant part of the underlying explanation for the apparent drift and loss of coherence of the church and the consequent loss of interest of the new generations. I have felt this for a number of years and I am by no means alone in it. For example, a few years ago I attended a three day get-together at my old seminary. At lunch on the final day I was discussing the church's troubles in a general way with one of my former classmates, now a solicitor. Drawing a bow at a venture, I said that things would not be sorted out until the church had digested and incorporated the thoughts of de Chardin. My classmate lowered his knife and fork and gave me a deliberate, solicitor-like look. Then, rather to my surprise, he simply said, "I agree" and went on with his lunch.

Contrary to any impression that may have been given, this whole chapter has not been one long whinge about the Christian church in general and the Catholic church in particular. The Christian church in general and the Catholic church in particular abound with dedicated, loving men and women trying with might and main to do whatever needs to be done. But what is to be done? When one looks at the church one sees a bustle of committees, meetings, ministries, good causes and so on. Everyone seems so busy. It is a frantic antheap. Viewed over a perspective of years, Vatican II seems to have turned away from the old direction of advance and not yet found a new one. The contents of this chapter so far have been material to illustrate this and its consequences. Vatican II was forced on the church by the need to come forward mentally from medieval time and find an accommodation with the *status quo* of the twentieth century. All the vast discoveries of science over the centuries could no longer be ignored by the church; they needed to be absorbed, incorporated and located in a new overall perspective and way ahead. I submit that this has not yet been achieved. There is indeed the emphasis on the two commandments of love, but then there always was – nobody has put it better than Paul did nearly 2,000 years ago! That does not in itself bring an accommodation with the twentieth and twenty-first centuries. Much has been written – very much – but it is no good expecting the man in the pew to pick out how everything hangs together from several thousand pages of rolling periods. It has to be put clearly and pithily so that it can be readily comprehended with no misunderstanding. The message must be one with which the scientific facts are evidently compatible or it will not convince. The effort must be made to marry evolutionary history and scientific progress into the framework of religion. We were given a parson's nose at the outset by a first chapter of Genesis that set out the story of the Big Bang and the progress of evolution up to the coming of man thousands and thousands of years before this was all reached by science. Right in the 20th century there has been another example of how it is all of one piece. I refer to the way in which the very different routes taken by Whitton and de Chardin arrived at the remarkably compatible ideas of metaconsciousness and hyper-personality. The groundwork has all been done: now it needs to be taken on board and explained succintly.

One thing that has not changed but which does with hindsight seem to have been misunderstood is the undimmed, absolute pre-eminence of God. We may remember that the Ten Commandments put this first, foremost and forcefully. That surely cannot change. The importance of man is merely in the context of this think-act. He is the leader in the Tree of Life, the leader in bringing the rise of consciousness to its completion. Man is important as the principal agent in furthering the development of this think-act: it is in this context that man has intrinsic value. Perhaps that sounds rather severe, but it is a perspective that scotches any thoughts of 'domesticating God'.

The old order was authoritarian and monolithic in its beliefs and interpretations of them. Monolithic is a particularly apt word as it brings to mind the associated expression 'set in concrete'. To change the metaphor to woodwork, everything was dovetailed in, making it extremely difficult to incorporate any new knowledge or new thinking. It was the strains imposed by this that gave rise to the need for Vatican II. Unfortunately, what predictably happened was that the old order had become an edifice so full of inbuilt strains that attempts to modify any part of it led to major structural collapses. The old self-confident authoritarian order disappeared but there was no new order ready developed and waiting to be put over to the man in the pew that embraced, accommodated, incorporated and used all the knowledge gained in recent times. It was as if the church knew that it had to accommodate the advance of science and of man's knowledge but did not know how to do so. There was no new cosmic vision ready to replace the old vision that man's knowledge had outgrown and which was visibly beginning to crack like a snake skin about to be sloughed off. Thirty years on from Vatican II the picture is just as woolly for the man in the pew. The only person to my knowledge who has made a comprehensive attempt to marry the advances in scientific knowledge into an overall Christian philosophic vision is de Chardin. His work may need to be clarified, updated and amended, but to my knowledge it is the only such work in existence. That is why it is of such crucial importance. Concepts like the Big Bang, space-time, evolution, the no-osphere and Omega need to be faced by institutional Christianity then digested and used by it. Until this happens there will continue to be a wilderness occupied by the empty crumbling shells of abandoned ideas. It is in this philosophical wasteland that humanist triumphalism has flourished to the extent that the Bishop of London was made to feel the need to talk about attempts to domesticate God. Nature hates a vacuum. It is only when the knowledge gained by the natural sciences has been incorporated as part of a total vision such as that of de Chardin that the still latent promise of Vatican II can be fulfilled.

CONCLUSION

What would you say now, O Euthyphro, in answer to Socrates's question, "What is goodness?". What answer will you give to Socrates? Has this essay at coherence been of any help to you?

The answer might go something like this. "Well, Socrates, my original answer was not so far off track as it seemed, as it turns out that there is only one God after all. So if we are looking for goodness we can indeed look to see what is pleasing to God, what God wants. Up to now the emphasis seems to have been on evolution so in general terms we might say that that thing is good which furthers the progress of evolution. It has often been violent, savage and cruel. But we are now on the cusp. We are at the turn of the tide. In about 400 years time – the mere twinkling of an eye in historical terms – the signal will be given to change to a more advanced priority, that of involution. What I will have to suggest for goodness for the future – with the proviso that it is necessary to preserve what has been achieved by evolution and not destroy it – is that that thing is good which furthers the progress of involution."

How have we arrived at this? I have made an essay at coherence and this meant that I had to begin with fundamentals outside this 'bank and shoal of time'. There are so many discussions and debates held that are obviously never going to come to any final resolution because the view is too restricted. I know that Aristotle said that we must work from our experience, but I would submit that this does not exclude consideration of things that are outside space-time, because we can argue from things which are in our experience. When I throw down two pennies and they lie on the floor immobile, this is something within my experience; but the laws of motion which eventually come to light from a study of this lead me back to an Immoveable Mover, who is patently not contained within space-time. A lot of the hobbled debates about science and religion and philosophy currently in vogue make me think of two men wandering in a thick fog on the side of a mountain arguing passionately about what the view spread out below them must look like. Astronomers have calculated that the Big Bang with which space-time started in a flash when Subsistent Being said, "Let there be light" happened something like 15 billion years ago. Space-time is patently not firm enough ground in which to anchor an essay at coherence. I had to start outside it. All the causes in our universe are secondary causes. You can add up, multiply and compound secondary causes until you are blue in the face but they will never turn into a primary uncaused cause. You can postulate parallel universes or cyclical universes that start from a Big Bang and eventually implode on themselves ready for another Big Bang to your hearts content but it will never explain where the original power came from. It is not reasonable to look to secondary causes for a complete answer. My search for firmer ground on which to anchor the thesis led me from considerations of motion, causality and contingency to the absolute of Subsistent Being, the non-contingent Prime Cause. This first uncaused cause contains 'virtually' all that can possibly be. Subsistent Being is infinite, simple, one, personal, perfect, eternal, omniscient and omnipotent. Moreover, from our experience it seems that existence is congruent with activity. Even the rocks in the garden, which seem to lie there passive and unmoving, are seething with myriads of frantically active electrons. So an infinite God will be infinitely and eternally active. When you think of infinity, our own Big Bang is pretty small beer. The whole universe at whose vastness we marvel is literally infinitesimal – it makes not a whit of difference to the infinity of Subsistent Being. There always seems to have been a worry among churchmen over pantheists who might claim that God was no more than the sum of all this our universe. If they were worried about this then they simply had not taken on board and inwardly digested their own avowed belief in the infinity of God. On the other side of the coin, if the pantheists really believed that all the bits of this universe in space-time added up to God then their thinking was culpably shallow.

I have to admit that my framework, in what purports to be an essay at coherence, has been rather higgledy-piggledy. After considering the absolute of Subsistent Being I turned in the introductory establishment of parameters to the Bible as the record of Man's dealings with God. I wanted to say that I found it reasonable to accept it as a historical record much as I would accept the work of Xenophon or Caesar. Then I was ready to return to the main stream and make the first suggestion of my own, that of the concept of the THINK-ACT. One of the problems of coming to grips with the contents of space-time for us humans has always been the division into material and immaterial, form and essence, mind and material objects, 'things in themselves' and 'appearances'. This is a problematic division that we are always aware of; we are always aware of the limits on the physical movement of our bodies, the limits of our psychic interaction with other people, the fact that we cannot transport ourselves at will, the fact that we are not able to merge our thoughts with the thoughts of those round about us and so on. Well, that is *our* problem. The shortcoming is ours; it is a limitation of the way we are made. It is not, however, a limitation to restrict almighty and omniscient Subsistent Being, which contains everything 'virtually' within itself. Our small problems over mind and matter simply do not apply. They are just divisions made within the framework of this our space-time by the power that made it. I thus came to postulate the think-act, suggesting that for Subsistent Being thought and action are inseparable and that every thought of Subsistent Being is a think-act.

Having thus established a perspective, it was then, and only then, the right juncture to go into space-time and examine it as one of, probably, an infinite number of multifarious think-acts of Subsistent Being. I looked at the path of evolution from the first flash of manifestation of the energy of the think-act and the establishment of space-time entailed in this, the transition from particles to atoms, to molecules, to polymers, to cells with the advent of life, and the progression through the variegated forms of the Tree of Life with increasing cerebralisation culminating with the advent of thought at the level of reflective consciousness in Man. This is the era of the survival of the fittest, the era of Nature red of tooth and claw. The two great driving forces, the two universal natural laws, were those of self-preservation and reproduction. In following the story of evolution through it became evident that it was the story of increasing complexification and ultimately the story of increasing cerebrelisation, the story of the rise of consciousness culminating at last in reflective consciousness in man.

I think that my second genuinely original input into this work is a suggested explanation of the dichotomy between the Old Testament and the New Testament. This is something which I have never heard attempted from the pulpit and it is one, indeed, that a local ecumenical Christian study group abandoned as being too difficult. The Old Testament is a story riddled with slaughter, rapine and treachery that appears irreconcilable with the precepts contained in the New Testament. It is, I submit, the story of life during the epoch of the hegemony of evolution. The Bible begins with a pithy but breathtakingly factually correct narrative of the sequence of evolution from the Big Bang up to the advent of Man. With Abraham it becomes the story of the relationship of a particular group of men with God from the very earliest times until they had reached a high level of civilisation. The high levels of civilisation achieved by several large groups of humans by the time of the coming of Christ could not have been attained without rules better than those of the natural law of the survival of the fittest and and opportunist procreation. These laws are too violent and selfish to allow harmonious development of any but the smallest groupings. They had to be modified and codified to allow the large, stable groupings necessary as the take-off platforms for higher civilisation. The Old Testament is about the race chosen by God for his favour in this evolutionary development stage and their laws were given to them directly by God in the Decalogue, the Ten Commandments. The first part of these laws was a requirement to acknowledge and pay deference to God and the second part contained the basic rules for the maintenance of social stability and harmony.

160

Of course, as evolution reached the stage of very large civilisations there were the beginnings of involution: but we must not lose sight of the fact that the human stage of this process is very short in historical terms. The Big Bang was something like 15 billion years ago; we are only talking in terms of millions of years since the coming of the earliest anthropoid forms; and we are only talking of the previous 10,000 years, the time since agriculture developed after the last Ice Age, when we are talking of the rise of civilisation. Historically speaking, this last part is microscopically short. Nevertheless, the tide was on the turn and when the time was ripe there occurred what was quite literally the single most epoch-making event in the whole of history, the event that occasioned the changeover of notation from BC to AD, the coming of Christ.

I submit that the coming of Christ marks the change from the primacy of evolution to that of the primacy of involution. Perhaps I may be the first to put this contention forward in these terms, but I do not claim originality for myself in thinking it out. The heavy thinking was done by de Chardin. It may not be stated quite so explicitly, but I believe that the idea is implicit in the sum of his writings as a scientist and as a priest. The signal for this change from emphasis on the radial and evolutionary to emphasis on the tangential and involutionary was contained in the two new commandments of love, which carried forward the 'thou shalt not' of the Decalogue into the 'thou shalt' of the Christian age. It was not a cancellation but a carrying forward, a fulfilment of what had gone before. (The new commandments of love are explained at length, eloquently and with great clarity in the introductory section to the Papal Encyclical *Veritatis Splendor*, which was published just as I came to draft this final chapter.)

I looked not only at why Christ came and why he came when he did but also at who he was. I found it reasonable to accept that he was the incarnation of Subsistent Being, the physical port of entry of God as a partaker in the events of the space-time that he made for his own good will and pleasure, not just as originator and director but as a

161

human being, not as the ethereal flames that did not consume the burning bush but as a mortal man.

Moving on to love and involution brought me to the no-osphere, the word coined by de Chardin to describe the immaterial equivalent of such tangible things as the geosphere, hydrosphere, atmosphere and biosphere.I wrote about the L-fields researched by men like Burr and touched on the T-fields. Strangely enough, people seem to have a powerful hang-up about accepting that anything can be real unless they can detect and measure it. This is one of the problems endemic in restricting our view to space-time. I made the point that matter and detectable energy were merely transient manifestations of the power of Subsistent Being. Fundamental, underlying reality is not – cannot be – limited to such contingent, transient things. They are no more than effects of it.

I took a look at near death experiences (NDEs) and some of the statements made by patients of Dr Whitton during hypnotic regression when he apparently caught them in a discarnate state between lives. While I do not believe that there is reincarnation and life between lives, I see no reason why it may not be possible during hypnotic regression to tap into deeper and deeper levels of the collective unconscious of the no-osphere. What really fascinated me was the similarity in the reports of these people who found themselves in a state of light, happiness, peace and love. While Jung and Whitton based their observations on the people who were the subjects of their clinical work and professional research, de Chardin (although I expect he was familiar with Jung) developed his idea of the no-osphere from deductions extrapolated from his scientific work and observations. The astounding thing is that his pursual of mega-synthesis and hyper-personality arrived by pure reason at something very akin to what Whitton described as meta-consciousness, where the subjects were aware of the All while still being acutely aware of themselves as persons. This point where all consciousness and all the conscious come together was named the Omega Point by de Chardin and it is the culmination of the rise of consciousness.

162

It struck me that it is much easier for us to come to grips with the notion of the human psyche and the no-osphere thanks to our familiarity with computers. I found this analogy very helpful and it makes it all the more amazing to me to realise that de Chardin produced his epoch-making thesis purely by abstract thought. He is the one modern philosopher to have attempted a universal synthesis and I salute him.

In the course of the essay up to this point I had floated some thoughts on the Resurrection, trinity and unity, reincarnation, the soul and the body. As a sort of philosophical coda I wrote down some ideas on hell and freewill. These various ideas may be helpful or provocative or trivial or controversial or infuriating, but if they provide some food for thought and stimulate other abler minds to develop them or to put forward alternatives then that is all to the good. I also postulated the need to reappraise the whole doctrine of the Atonement in view of the insecurity of its basis in the story of Adam and Eve, the Garden of Eden and the Fall.

At the outset I bemoaned the fact that not only philosophers but also theologians seemed to have lost impetus in this modern age of scientific wonders; and in the last chapter before this Conclusion I turned to the state of the Christian churches. Vatican II was convened because the Catholic church was seen to be becoming more and more archaic in appearance and presentation of its message in relation to the modern world. The strains were showing. Good Pope John wanted to open the doors and windows and let the fresh air in: unfortunately, when the doors and windows were opened the most conspicuous result was that many of the congregation went out. The falling away of the young has been particularly startling. Indeed, I have heard a clergyman refer to Confirmation as 'the leaving certificate'. I outlined how the result of the Conference, as seen from the pew, appeared to be disunity, demoralisation, loss of certainty, retreat from contentious issues and a huge outpouring of lengthy documents written in high-flown language which utterly failed to give an exciting, inspiring renewal of purpose and vision of the way ahead

163

such as might be taken up by the faithful with shouts of acclamation and a fiery enthusiasm. The metaphor that comes unbidden to mind is rather that of a 'damp squib'. As yet.

Clear, sure ideas require few words. The two new commandments of love, the Eight Beatitudes, the Our Father are good examples; so is the Creed; so was the Penny Red. This last covered the whole of Christian doctrine in 72 little pages 5 ins. x 3_ ins. (I feel sure that its authors could have set out the bull points of *Veritatis Splendor* in question and answer format on one page of A4). Yet how much was often packed into one short sentence! Take, for example, the answer to Question 2, 'Why did God make you?'. The answer given is 'God made me to know Him, love Him and serve Him in this world and to be happy with Him for ever in the next'. I would just like to pause over 'to *serve* Him'. In days long gone by there was much preaching about keeping oneself untouched by the world and of this world being no more than an ante-chamber of eternity, worthy of no consideration on its own account. Yet in the Penny Red we have the germ of a vision of an intrinsic purpose to our life here on earth. This is developed at length by de Chardin in *Le Milieu Divin* in two large sections entitled 'The Divinisation of Our Activities' and 'The Divinisation of Our Passivities'. It is largely a very full exposition of my Commandment 3A (or was it 11?), 'Thou shalt not take thy football home': on the contrary, we must boot it about with vigour all over the pitch in eager participation in the game of this think-act. Not that it is written in such a vein! *Le Milieu Divin* is scholarly, reverent and lovely. I commend it for personal reading. I said earlier that I felt that the key to the triumphant fulfilment of the aims of Vatican II lay in the ideas of this learned and saintly man. In the past 30 years there has been a strong emphasis on the intrinsic importance of man and of the here and now, but it seems to have turned out to be at the expense of deference to God because the essential reason for the importance of mankind as being the lead shoot of the Tree of Life, carrying the prime responsibility for furthering involution to completion at the Omega Point, has not been used to put things in perspective. If Vatican II is seen as a regrouping ready for the final journey to Omega then the importance of mankind and the world is placed in context. Our importance lies in our work to bring about the *Milieu Divin.*

In taking a universal perspective from the viewpoint of a theologian and a modern scientist, de Chardin incorporated much modern material and thinking, notably that stemming from the ideas of Darwin. I have tried to draw in also some ideas from men like Jung, Einstein, Burr and Whitton with the aim of making an essay at coherence compatible with both theology and science based on the grand vision of de Chardin, whose writings (or, more precisely, the difficulty of whose writings) were responsible for setting the whole project in motion. If anybody thinks that I am barking up the wrong tree I would only ask him not to waste his energies negatively in taking my work to pieces but to take the positive course of sitting down and writing his own essay at coherence, showing things as they should be. We need the knowledge gained by analysis to be gathered up and the vision of synthesis, mega-synthesis, to be developed and filled out. There is certainly plenty of scope for new work in this field: apart from the trail-blazing work of de Chardin it is pretty much a blank sheet.